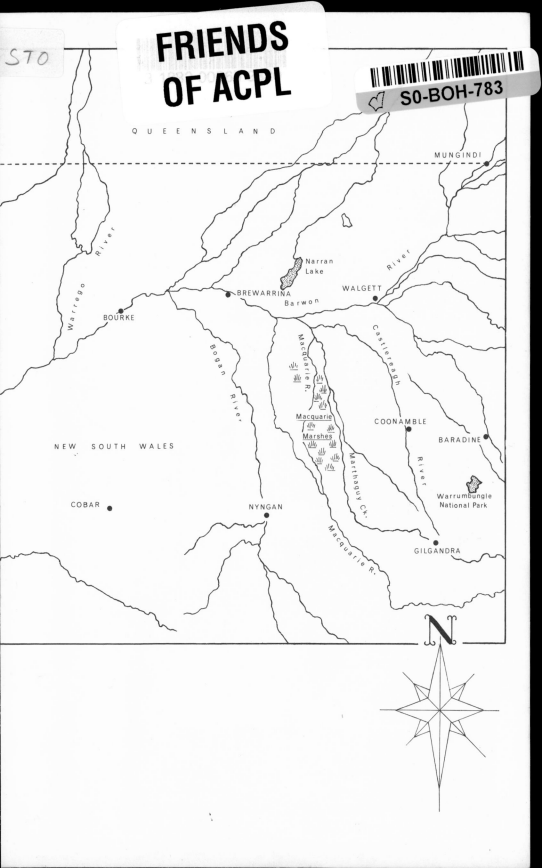

QUEENSLAND

MUNGINDI

Warrego River

Narran
Lake

River

BREWARRINA

WALGETT

Barwon

BOURKE

Bogan River

Macquarie R.

Castlereagh

Macquarie
Marshes

COONAMBLE

River

BARADINE

NEW   SOUTH   WALES

Marthaguy Ck.

Warrumbungle
National Park

COBAR

NYNGAN

Macquarie R.

GILGANDRA

N

11·11·77

The Year of the Kangaroo

Also by H. D. Williamson

The Year of the Koala

The Year of the Kangaroo

H. D. Williamson
Illustrated by Roy B. Doyle

Charles Scribner's Sons NEW YORK

Copyright © 1977 Henry Williamson

Library of Congress Cataloging in Publication Data

Williamson, Henry Darvall.
The year of the kangaroo.

Bibliography: p. 177
Includes index.
1. Kangaroos.   I. Title.
QL795.K3W53   599'.2   77-13362
ISBN 0-684-15187-1

1 3 5 7 9 11 13 15 17 19 V|C 20 18 16 14 12 10 8 6 4 2
Printed in the United States of America

Contents

1982363

Preface

So many Australian animals are unusual that it seems inevitable that some of them should be controversial as well. Consider the kangaroo, for instance. What an extraordinarily unconformable creature, not only in appearance but in habit! Leaving aside the pros and cons of the subject, is it any wonder that men find it exasperating that a fence quite adequate for the restraint of sheep and cattle may be no more than a temporary check to a kangaroo?

Everyone, surely, can sympathize with the farmer who discovers that a mob of kangaroos has raided his wheat field overnight and, having eaten a little of it, has then lounged and lazed over a great deal more before making off again at dawn.

Except in those areas where kangaroos exist in sizable numbers the big landholders, or graziers, who farm sheep or cattle on a large scale are not as severely affected. But they have their difficulties, too.

Yet one of the most wonderful sights of natural Australia

is a company of red kangaroos bounding over the plains. Or, for that matter, a lone red buck or blue flyer suddenly sitting up to stare suspiciously at an approaching car or man on horseback.

Fortunately, there are many landowners who are appreciative of such things, and the fate of many of our free-roaming animals may well rest with them. Not that there is not a host of problems, some of which will be explored in the following pages.

There is at least one point in the controversy that has become abundantly clear—however much most Australians may admire kangaroos, it simply is not just to refer to farmers and graziers in accusing terms. The question is too complicated for that. Nor will a solution miraculously appear; it will have to be sought.

What is needed most now is information, for it is not until we know more about kangaroos that we can decide how best to manage them.

Of course there are always the wildlife reserves, and probably some species will survive only in these. But there seems no reason why a certain proportion of kangaroos cannot continue to exist alongside sheep and cattle—and men—in acceptable numbers on some Australian properties.

Four species of kangaroo are described in *The Year of the Kangaroo*: the red kangaroo (*Megaleia rufa*); the great gray or eastern gray kangaroo, which is also known as the forester (*Macropus giganteus*); the western gray or mallee kangaroo (*Macropus fuliginosus*); and the hill kangaroo, euro or wallaroo (*Macropus robustus*).

These are all large kangaroos. Besides other species of

large kangaroos there are many smaller species ranging in size from wallabies and rock wallabies down to pademelons, hare wallabies, and rat kangaroos.

Because of the extra amount of grass that has become available through the clearing of land and the provision of more drinking points, the larger kangaroos have generally maintained or increased their numbers. Even so, the red kangaroo is a rare sight now in those parts of the country where a policy of closer settlement has resulted in much grazing land being turned into plowed fields. As an offset to this there are more red kangaroos in the back country, especially in Queensland. It is the smaller species of the forests and scrubs that have suffered so disastrously, and the only hope for their survival seems to be the national park. But small kangaroos do not come within the scope of this narrative.

The Year of the Kangaroo is made up of facts gathered by various means and arranged and presented in fictional form to give continuity. Work carried out by trained scientists—lengthy and painstaking work—is the broad biological base that supports most of our knowledge of wild creatures, although observation of each separate subject in its native state is necessary, too. The experiences of rangers, graziers, farmers, and kangaroo shooters are therefore invaluable, and any writer who would describe an animal must spend hours of watching through a good pair of binoculars if a reasonable degree of verisimilitude is to be achieved.

As a rule red kangaroos are not difficult to observe. Provided the watcher approaches them carefully and does not try to get too close, they will not put themselves to the trouble of moving. If the watcher, having taken up his position, then stays still enough for long enough, the red kangaroos will obligingly forget his existence.

There is no substitute for watching wild creatures in their own habitats, although some information may be gained, too, from observing them when they are under constraint in parks and zoos. But under the latter conditions some reservations often have to be made in any conclusions that may be drawn.

It is amazing how quickly animals are affected by being caged. Some grow terrified, but most of them soon seem to realize—though what form the "realization" takes, who can say?—that the barrier that prevents them from getting out also keeps predators from getting in.

Let the lions roar when the keeper is late with their food, their thunderous fury is of no more significance than the whisper of the wind in the wire netting to the gazelles in the next enclosure.

Sightseers snap their fingers at, and make rude remarks about, some timid herbivore which has gone to sleep and will not budge from its place in the sun. It has become so used to the endless stream of humans shuffling past its pen that it cannot be roused into even blinking its heavy-lidded eyes.

So the visitors move on and never see big red poised for flight or standing up to his full height to gaze into the distance, never see the blue flyer's electric leap from danger or two bucks battling over a doe—especially the last. Zoo specimens are valuable and any quarrelsome buck is quickly separated from the rest and sold.

So the information in any narrative of the lives of wild

creatures comes from many sources. For this book the sources include works like *Kangaroos*, by H. J. Frith and J. H. Calaby, isolated experiments, wildlife rangers, men on the land, kangaroo shooters and bushmen generally, as well as personal observation.

In writing *The Year of the Kangaroo* I have referred often to Allan M. Fox, the chief education officer of the National Parks and Wildlife Service, who, besides being an authority on kangaroos, has an extraordinary knowledge of the associated subjects from native trees and grasses, through climate, topography, and geology, and back to most kinds of Australian fauna and the principles of conservation. He has read much of the manuscript, and his advice has been invaluable. My thanks are due also to Edward P. Finnie, who is the head veterinarian at the Taronga Park Zoo in Sydney, to Dave Thomas, the head keeper of marsupials at the same zoo, to Bill Brown of Cobar, and to Ron McMillan, kangaroo shooter of Coonamble.

During one of my visits to confer with Dave Thomas, a lively incident occurred. He told me he had become identified as a rival by a red kangaroo buck sharing an enclosure with some blue flyers and their joeys (young kangaroos). This kangaroo showed signs of belligerence whenever Dave appeared and was at its best, or worst, depending on the point of view, early in the morning.

I met Dave at the Zoo early one morning and we made for the marsupial section. Catching sight of us while we were some distance away, the kangaroo immediately went into its threat routine and was really acting up by the time we reached it. We watched for a minute or two, and then as Dave was about to open the gate the animal bounced toward him, not swiftly but menacingly, making clutching movements with the sharp, curved talons of its front paws.

Needless to say, we kept the gate shut. It was just as well that the kangaroo had worked itself up to such a pitch of aggression during our approach and had attacked before the gate was opened; otherwise Dave would have had a very unpleasant experience.

The aboriginal names used to distinguish two of the kangaroos in the narrative are Wangarie and Merloo. Wangarie means "pretty face" and is also an alternative name in English for the southern whiptail (*Macropus parryi*) or pretty-face wallaby. As the markings on the muzzle of the southern whiptail, or pretty-face, bear some resemblance to the black whisker marks on the creamy-white muzzle of the female red kangaroo, or blue flyer, the name Wangarie is quite appropriate. Merloo, the name given to one of Wangarie's joeys, means simply "red kangaroo."

In a book of this kind where each of the twelve chapters is headed by the name of a month, it is well for the reader in the northern hemisphere to bear in mind that spring in Australia occurs in September, October, and November, summer in December, January, and February, autumn in March, April, and May, and winter in June, July, and August. Of course there is no great variation among the seasons in Australia, and an occasional sunny day in mid-winter may be quite as warm as a mild day in mid-summer.

Finally, all Roy Doyle's illustrations except two are of

red kangaroos—red bucks, blue flyers, and joeys. The exceptions are the illustration for April, which depicts a young gray forester buck taking a grass seed from near its eye by using the twin claws of its hind foot, and the illustration for November, which is of a wallaroo.

The Year of the Kangaroo

January

IT IS NOON, and hot, along the foothills of the Great Divide. Around Baradine, where the level grasslands begin, a prolonged dry spell is fast turning into drought.

The only interruptions to the sweep of the plains westward are the trees, small, infrequent trees, most of them solitary. Sometimes the trees seem to be only tricks of the light; they sway like flames in the heat haze or vanish altogether for a while, as those in the distance often do.

Seven kangaroos are drowsing in the shade of a stand of wilgas. They have been camping there long enough now to have scooped out a number of shallow depressions, and it is their habit of lying in these that makes them as inconspicuous as a scatter of flattish rocks—provided they do not move. But they are a restless lot, somnolent but restless, and there is nearly always a head, black against the glare, craning up to take an observation, or a forepaw tossing dust into the air to keep away the flies.

The biggest of the kangaroos, a red buck, is leaning on

his elbow. A blue flyer, likewise propped on an elbow but with her paws crossed in front of her, is nodding, then waking up, then nodding off again, and so on. Her slim hind legs, as pale as those of the yearling buck beside her, are powerful and full of grace. As she dozes there her long, equine ears are always on the alert. Even when she seems to be fast asleep her ears will flick to dislodge a fly; and they are continually turning, generally together but sometimes independently, as they traverse the quiet for sounds.

Abruptly, the old buck raises the front part of his body and stares fixedly into the distance. His ears are pricked. If he wants to hold his head any higher he will have to exert himself further, and he is not sure that further exertion will be necessary so he remains as he is, at gaze.

But there is nothing to see out there except an afternoon mirage of a blue lake. Everywhere else is brown earth. While the buck listens the deep rose powdering on his throat and upper chest catches the light and gleams like blood against the rufous-tinted undersurfaces of his body.

The other kangaroos, at first disturbed by his sharp movement, settle down again. Then abruptly, the second full-grown buck bounces to his feet. He matured only last year, and his coat lacks the rich color of his companion's, but he is a fine sight nevertheless as he stretches up to balance on the tripod of his hind toes and tail. Tense and ready to go, he peers in the direction of the almost inaudible humming of a land rover crossing the station property by a back track, probably making for the Coonamble-Baradine road. No other member of the group troubles to bestir a limb, although every ear has now pivoted toward the same point. Then the sound starts to recede.

Bending his head, with its whitish muzzle and black streaks, the old buck licks his forearms. He licks them until they are dark with saliva and then closes his eyes to drowse again while the evaporation cools and soothes him. The younger buck drops to his paws and noses at the ground. With his weight on his fore and hind feet, he draws his great tail under him and, using it as a third limb, allows his body and hind legs to swing easily forward, pendulum fashion. He nuzzles one of the does in passing then flops down again, scratches his chest noisily, and goes to sleep. It is quiet—except every now and then there is a convulsive jump as a fly stings one of the group and up will go a paw and yet another spurt of dust. By this hour of late afternoon every one of the resting animals, including an immature male of fourteen months and a female of about the same age, is sprinkled with dirt, dead wilga leaves, and bits of stick. So far the two young-at-heel have left the scattering of debris to their elders. The male is rather larger than the female, but both are undersized because of the droughty season. Gangling, slab-sided little creatures with long hind legs as slim as antelopes', they have a listlessness about them which is the result of lack of food. They are less watchful than the older kangaroos and the things that periodically alarm them—the shadow of a hawk descending, the sudden, loud skirring of insects, the lizard that whisks under their noses—pass apparently unnoticed by the others.

As the rays of the sun reach under the trees, the various members of the group become more distinct. The big buck is not only taller, stronger, and heavier than any of the others but is obviously much older. He is, in fact, very old and his dark red fur, aflame in the sunset, bears the scars of many a battle and of half a hundred collisions with wire fences and fallen deadwood. A healed-up rent extending from his shoulder to almost the middle of his back shows where a greyhound's teeth missed his neck, a big patch of hair is missing from his tail, and a line through the lighter fur of his chest and belly is the nail mark of a rival's forward and downward slashing kick that failed to pierce his skin. Lumbering stiffly to his feet, he stares over the plains without looking at anything in particular. While his forepaws scratch at his chest he arches his back and yawns luxuriously, then drops on his front legs exactly as the younger buck had done and swings his great weight forward on the tripod of his front legs and tail. Drenched in heat and sleep, he has scarcely moved since morning, and it is almost possible to hear his sinews creaking and to feel the twinges of pain that rack him as he again swings forward and noses the ground, finding nothing. After three of these moves, a mode of progress that could be more aptly likened to that of a man on crutches than the bounding of a kangaroo, he sits up on his haunches, motionless. When one of the youngsters—the female—in an impulsive, sprightly whirl around the wilgas, accidentally bumps into him he lets go a backhander that would have sent her flying had it connected. The discomfort of getting his aged frame into working order has not improved his temper. It has been pretty bad for years, and he will probably become a solitary before long.

The members of the group differ amazingly in size and general appearance. Their absolute colors are the dark, rich red of the old buck and the misty blueness of the blue flyers with, for the younger animals, any shade that can be

produced by the blending of red and blue in varying proportions. Farther west, toward the center of Australia, there
is the added complication that the bucks are sometimes
blue and the females red.

Despite their differences in size and their many color
variations, however, all the kangaroos under the wilga
trees belong to the same species, *Megaleia rufa*, the red
kangaroo—although it is no wonder that the little blue
flyers are often mistaken for wallabies. Weighing nearly
ninety-five kilograms, the biggest of the three bucks is
more than three and one-half times heavier than
Wangarie.

At least the group is consistent in that its members con-
form to the rules that apply to the region, for Wangarie is
as blue as any animal of the species could possibly be, and
the biggest buck is as red. At nearly two and one-quarter
meters tall, he towers over the blue flyers, especially when
he stands up on his toes and the end of his tail to stare into
the distance. All the kangaroos have black whisker patches
shading toward the eyes, and Wangarie is particularly well
marked in this way, the intensely black streaks on her face
contrasting strongly with the whitish sides of her muzzle.
When she gets to her feet she does so lithely, the bulge in
her pouch showing she is carrying a joey that is not yet a
heavy burden.

Of the other blue flyers the younger has a reddish tinge,
but the elder is almost as blue as Wangarie; while, oppo-
sitely, the younger of the mature bucks, though generally
red, has enough blue left in the fur of his forehead, neck,
and the butt of his tail to make those parts quite definitely
mauve.

The temperature has dropped a few degrees since noon,

but there is no freshness about the evening. Yet the glare of the day has gone and the bleached-out whiteness of the sky has deepened to an intense blue. A raven in lonely flight is so high that the beat of its wings is just discernible.

All the kangaroos are stirring. Spurts of dust, golden in the sun, spring up as the two young-at-heel join in a last, wild gambol before the group starts to leave; then the female stops her caperings and hops through the rest of the company to be near her mother. But Wangarie takes no notice of her. Her daughter, although no longer being suckled, will remain at heel for another six to twelve months, since the dry season has delayed her development.

When another blue flyer stands up the number of animals in sight increases to eight, then diminishes again to seven as the joey who has been hidden against her side dives into her pouch.

The plains are yellow and black in streaks and blotches. There are no mirages now, no illusory blue lakes to hide the stricken earth as the horizon flames like the rim of the sun itself and goes out.

The drought in the west has been like a bushfire, leaving the country exhausted, the stock dead. Many of the wild creatures, too, have died. Others, such as the kangaroos, have fled before it into paddocks where there is yet some feed. Since then it has been raining in the far west but the intervening desolation is too wide for them to cross. Here, at the foot of the Warrumbungles, there have also been thunderstorms, and it seems the region will be spared the worst.

The red kangaroos move through the dusk. Their order

is haphazard but, by chance, the aged buck—a boomer, if ever there was one—leads. He will be passed by all the others if they travel far that night. He could make the going easier if he could increase his speed sufficiently to get some rhythm into his gait. The length of each of his hops is so short that most of his effort goes into lifting his great weight off the ground with very little left for shifting it along. Nor will his aging muscles be hurried.

Soon, the oldest of the flyers passes him, swinging by at a fair pace on the hugely developed toes of her hind feet. She is going fast enough for her counterbalancing tail and short forelimbs never once to brush the ground, and she seems to find the weight of the well-grown joey, who is looking out of her pouch, a trifling burden, although he must be nearly big enough to be making his own way. In any case, the boomer could never move like that—he never has, for that matter, although he will do better when he has limbered up.

Wangarie is wide and to the side. The head and rabbit ears of her five-month-old joey are protruding from her pouch also, and her older offspring is hopping along beside her. Sometimes, in shying at shadows in the gathering dark, the small doe-at-heel blunders into her parent and once is knocked sprawling. But she is on her feet again in a moment. The third and youngest blue flyer, whose pouched young is about the size of a mouse, is bounding easily along beside the young buck. Last of all is her fourteen-month-old young-at-heel—last, that is, until he skirts around the boomer in a burst of speed and comes up alongside his mother. As they journey on, the apparent cohesion among them breaks up and they spread out.

They are close enough, however, to make a concentrated thumping sound that could be heard in the stillness at a distance of about a hundred meters from the nearest animal.

Although the mob is moving slowly, the old buck gradually drops farther behind, and he continues to lose ground even after he has settled into his usual traveling gait.

As a rule kangaroos are loath to abandon their daytime sleeping places in summer, especially if they have been centered under some shady trees long enough to have scooped out hollows for their hip bones. They will sometimes travel two or three kilometers to feed rather than shift camp. On this occasion, however, the seven have already passed all the spots where they have foraged recently, so it becomes increasingly likely that they are making for a new area.

It is only by persistent searching that they will have a chance to outlast the drought, and it is only because they have been able to travel farther from water than cattle or sheep that they have managed to find an occasional patch of grass in gilgais and crab holes where rain collects during a storm. But mortality has already been severe, particularly among pouched young and young-at-heel, whether they are being suckled or not. So far, about half of these have died. The more advanced in development a joey is, the greater the risk of death from starvation, and the only sucklings at present sure of obtaining enough nourishment to keep them alive are the tiny creatures attached to the teat, their demands being, like themselves, infinitesimal. It is remarkable that the three mature does in the group should have two young-at-heel and three pouched young among them. The very small pouched young attached to the teat of the youngest of the three blue flyers is being adequately fed, but it is not certain that either of the others will survive, since one is almost due to leave the pouch and the other, Wangarie's joey, will be due to leave in about three weeks. Both of these, therefore, will be entering the most vulnerable stage of their existence already weakened by the partial failure of their parents' milk supply.

The seven are now at the extreme eastern limits of their range, and to go farther will be to enter the timbered country of the gray foresters and the tumbled steeps of the wallaroos—the hill kangaroos. So they veer back to the plains and almost blunder into some dogs tearing at the remains of a sheep. As the kangaroos again change direction the boomer gives a warning thwack with his hind feet and, urged on by this resounding alarm and an outburst of barking from the dogs, the rest of the group forges ahead of him.

There are four dogs and the fastest is a yellowish, half-breed greyhound. About a year ago she defected from a party of town huntsmen to become a scavenger around campsites in the foothills of the Warrumbungles and a killer of small game. Her mate is a black-and-white dog with a head like a bull terrier's. He spends most days sleeping outside a tumbledown hut on the Coonabarabran road. Sometimes the occupant of the hut throws him something to eat. On bright moonlight nights he goes hunting with the greyhound bitch. The remaining two dogs are fierce, thick-set, and slow. Like the others they are really feral dogs, although only the half-breed greyhound has no link left with man and his habitations.

The game they are hunting tonight is fast, much faster

than sheep, bandicoots, and rabbits, and there are no young-at-heel so small that they are unable to keep up. The boomer is the slowest, but even he is maintaining his lead—by tactics more than pace. He always heads for the roughest going, swishing through the tops of bushes and bounding over any deadwood or other litter that would force the dogs to go around or thread their way through. But soon there is no way for the old buck to go but across an open plain, and it is then that the greyhound catches up. The big kangaroo coughs angrily and slides to a stop in a cloud of dust. Already he is showing signs of distress. Nevertheless, he is a formidable figure as he towers on his hind toes, his back to a tree. Every now and then the talons of his forepaws glint in the moonlight and the corded sinews of his forearms stand out in relief. From somewhere ahead of the trio the crackling of dry debris tells of the does and young, still in flight.

Neither the yellow greyhound half-breed nor her black-and-white mate does more than menace the bailed-up boomer. He is too big and too dangerous to be pulled down without considerable risk to themselves. So they press on after the speedier kangaroos now traveling in a somewhat leisurely fashion along a sand ridge to get the benefit of softer landings.

Evidently the two heavier dogs have given up the chase altogether, for there is no sign of them, and the boomer soon resumes his ponderous way, following on behind the marauders. He enters the trees at the start of the same sand ridge the others are about to leave. The muffled impacts of his pads on the softer ground, the regular surge of his breathing, and an occasional crash as he lands in some fallen branches—the extra effort needed to clear them is not worth the trouble—are the only sounds he can hear at present.

However, the pursuers have gained a lot of ground on the dawdling blue flyers and their young-at-heel. They could have come still closer had the black-and-white dog not let out an excited yelp as he glimpsed the quarry flickering through the moonlight and shadows in front. Instantly, the fugitives split up. The six of them go in six different directions.

Wangarie, at full speed, races through the last of the trees, clears a fallen belah in a magnificent, sailing leap, and streaks across a cleared paddock dotted with sheep. She maintains her top pace for a while, then, finding she is not pursued, bounces warily to a stop and looks around, neck craned, ears pricked. Balancing on her toes and her tail's end, she is ready to go at the first hint of danger— well, the second hint, for she is a curious creature. But there is nothing in sight, nothing. Her daughter, who has been following her all night, has disappeared. So has every other member of the company.

Ignoring the two youngsters, though they would seem to be the easiest to run down, the dogs have given chase to the oldest of the blue flyers, and at present her lead is widening. They are literally eating up the distance, but the doe is drawing away. She is going at such a pace and so smoothly that she, too, seems to be running. Her lead increases as she recovers from the initial shock of finding the dogs so close, and she settles down to sheer speed. Her slim legs swing under her like power-driven pendulums, her head is as steady as an arrow in level flight, and the balancing movements of her tail are minimal. She is a blue flyer in full flight.

The quarry and both pursuers are now evenly spaced one behind the other, for just as the gap between kangaroo and greyhound is widening, so is the greyhound outstripping the black-and-white dog. Shadows flit across the blue flyer as she skirts a cluster of yarran, and the yellow gleam of the greyhound bitch is dimmed, too, before it flares again in the full moonlight. The fugitive is still drawing away.

But the doe is half-starved and the joey she might have carried another kilometer or more in a good season is already weighing her down. When she changes course toward a sand ridge dark with trees and littered with fallen branches, the greyhound cuts across to turn the maneuver against her—and the black-and-white dog comes into the picture again. Within moments the situation has altered completely, for the dogs are not only starting to press her but, heartened by the signs of her weakening, are finding the strength to run faster. She swerves at right angles and the greyhound springs for her throat, but misses and loses all the ground the flyer had given away by her deviation. Now neck and neck, the dogs are racing one on each side of her and only half a stride behind when, through terror or fatigue or conscious act, the muscles of her pouch relax and her joey tumbles out, sliding and rolling over and over in a mist of moonlit dust. Getting to his feet he sets off in erratic flight that expends as much effort in bobbing up and down as in making headway, and the greyhound gathers him in in a soundless rush. He is dead before the black-and-white dog arrives to chop a piece from his flank.

The blue flyer makes better speed, naturally, as soon as she is relieved of the weight of her offspring and, seeing no further threat, slows to a stop and looks around, exactly as Wangarie did. Almost exhausted, she waits awhile before licking her forearms to cool herself. Then she goes on, showing no awareness of her loss.

A kilometer or so away Wangarie has overtaken the red boomer, whose progress, though slow, has not included a frenzied dash in an opposite direction. However, he has now been stopped by a four-wire fence and has already spent time in trying to find a way around. Wangarie joins him in the hopeless quest. The boomer makes another attempt to go on as though there were nothing in front of him and is again thrown back. Both kangaroos have scrambled through or jumped over many such fences without ever being able to get the hang of them. They have often jumped higher obstacles, and there is not a shadow of a doubt that the old buck, and certainly the blue flyer, would have cleared this fence, too, with the greatest of ease if only it had been a darkly substantial barrier like a fallen tree or a heap of branches. But it is not, and, although its cobwebby filaments are no more worthy of notice than the tops of bushes or the long grass of a lush season, it will not let them pass.

It is Wangarie who finally pushes underneath. The fence is not netted, and the bottom wire twangs as her rounded back forces through. As she bounds away on the other side the boomer tries to follow but slams into the wires, where he is held. The wires sing as he fights them. But they do not break. And when the top part of him is through, his great hind legs are not. They have passed under the bottom wire and the rest of him is above it. He tries to bound away, nevertheless—and his forepart crashes to the ground. He panics. And when, eventually, he is through, a furrow has been clawed in the ground by his front paws in their strivings to haul him free, there are bloody patches on his haunches where he has been cut by the wire, and the fence has lost some of its tension. He makes off—ponderously, but at a good rate.

He goes on until the emptiness around him is suddenly peopled with a crowd of round-backed creatures. He stops but seems to take as little notice of the strangers as they do of him. The big mob of kangaroos is feeding where there has recently been a thunderstorm. The ground is pockmarked with gilgais and it is in these that the quicker-responding grasses have germinated. Wallaroos, gray foresters, and red kangaroos alike shave the new shoots close.

Although the stars and a slim moon now starting its descent to the west are dazzling when viewed from the ground, the light they shed on earth is so dim that nearly every one of the kangaroos seems to be gray, although, in fact, there are quite a few reds—mature bucks and blue does—dotted throughout the multitude. Most of the country surrounding the feeding ground is wooded and much of it is rolling country, hilly in parts and becoming more and more rugged toward the east. It is country that belongs to the gray forester and the wallaroo. Ordinarily, none of it would be inhabited by red kangaroos.

The three species of large kangaroos are concentrated in a relatively small space—but there are not many wallaroos. Wallaroos like to remain in their own scraps of territory, and those now in company with the reds and grays are easy to pick out.

They are as black as their own shadows and when they are hunched up, feeding, they look like boulders. It is when they sit up straight that the strength of their shaggy bodies and the thickness of their limbs are most apparent. Wallaroos can bound up the side of a gully as though it were level going. The old bucks are fierce fighters and likely to bail up without notice. They can be so truculent that challengers who continue to advance are often saved the exertion of going all the way and are risking a rough-house brawl with a tough and dirty antagonist who will not hesitate to use his teeth.

Feed is giving out in the new area, and on the afternoon following the arrival of Wangarie and the rest the kangaroos are not as numerous. Soon the grass is gone and so are the kangaroos. Some of the last to leave are the red kangaroos of the little company, whose numbers, omitting pouch young, have been restored to seven now that Wangarie's daughter-at-heel has rediscovered her mother.

Kangaroos, like most wild creatures, prefer to keep to animal paths, and as January comes to an end under cloudless, moonlit skies, in silence, airlessness, and heat, the group is traveling in single file along a track leading west.

February

THE BIG MOB that broke up during the last days of January is now so scattered that it is rare to find more than six or seven kangaroos together.

Despite the wide dispersion, however, the respective habitat preferences of the species remain apparent. The red kangaroos dislike the cypress belts and the scrubs where the gray foresters shelter by day, and the wallaroos never venture so far onto the plains that they cannot be back in their rocky hills on very short notice. The foresters, like the wallaroos, often visit the plains at night to feed, but only the reds roam them freely.

Wangarie and those behind her are lazing along a track that, having been pulverized by the hard little hoofs of sheep, is now recording the pad marks of the present travelers. Most of the prints are smudged, but the last of them are clear. These are the red boomer's, yet despite his great weight they are not much deeper than those made by the blue flyers.

Wangarie increases her pace until only her hind toes touch the ground, her trail a line of twin splashes in the dust. Her example sets them all going, and soon the seven are crawling under a fence near its corner—the boomer as usual having trouble getting through.

The night is silence and cataracts of stars. A wind as dry as the track the kangaroos have just left is blowing fitfully. Black as tree stumps, the kangaroos sit up on their haunches; their great ears turn, listening.

Drinking places are often dangerous, and it is Wangarie who goes on cautiously until the soil heaped around an earth tank looms like a range of faraway hills. Using the tripod method, she crawls up the mound and stops briefly when she sees the stars wavering in the wind-ruffled water. She and most of the other six edge cautiously down the slope to drink. Within minutes they are on their way again. The boomer is the last to leave because he was last to arrive, being warier than the others.

Threading their way through the cypress pines of a sand ridge, the kangaroos keep straight on across the plain. Small, shadowy forms glide away from the body of a gray forester, victim of the drought or a landholder's rifle, and the boomer utters a growling threat or two. The eyes of the foxes watching from a little distance are red points in the dark. Indifferent to both the sight and stench of death, the kangaroos explore the creek bed but find only a few dry stalks along its edges.

It is sunrise when the boomer lies down under a rose-wood tree. He is dead tired. The others go on to a strip of scrub where there is shelter enough for all of them.

The oldest of the blue flyers, whose joey was taken by

the dogs, has her back against a cypress and, with her tail stretched out in front of her so that she is really sitting, balanced, on the butt of it, starts to clean her pouch. The sun flares in the fur of her sides, the cypress trunk not being wide enough to shade her fully.

Although the period of gestation for a normal pregnancy is thirty-three days and the blue flyer has not mated for eight months, she is undoubtedly preparing for another birth. She is able to do this because of various elaborations in the strange pattern of reproduction in red kangaroos, not the least of which are the facts that the female red kangaroo, or blue flyer, has two uteri, the capacity to supply two different kinds of milk simultaneously, and a biological signaling system depending upon the sucking stimulus of her joey.

A joey is usually about seven months old when it starts leaving the maternal pouch for short periods to wander rather erratically about, to bask in the sun, and to do a little grazing on its own. This change of habit, including the beginnings of the weaning process, brings about a weakening of the sucking stimulus, which in turn causes the embryo waiting in the second of the female's uteri to resume development. The female's oestrous cycle, which has been suspended during the suckling of her joey, also starts again.

A sudden cessation of the sucking stimulus, as would occur if the empouched joey died prematurely, has the same effect as the more gradual weakening that eventually takes place when a joey lives long enough to start quitting the pouch for short intervals.

In those instances where the signal for the resumption of

the development of a dormant blastocyst is given by a progressive weakening of the sucking stimulus, the joey who has been venturing out of the pouch is able to use the thirty-one days—while his successor is developing—to become just that much bigger and closer to being fully weaned. By the time the next joey arrives he should be sufficiently mobile to cope with permanent exclusion from his mother's pouch.

A couple of days after her new joey is born, a blue flyer comes into oestrus again and mates. As her pouch now contains another suckling, the blastocyst from the mating will enter a dormant stage. This phenomenon is known as embryonic diapause.

If, as sometimes happens, a blue flyer becomes pregnant when she has no suckling in her pouch, the embryo does not enter a dormant phase—there is no sucking to induce it—and the gestation period proceeds uninterruptedly for its full thirty-three days, as distinct from the thirty-one days needed to complete development after embryonic diapause.

None of the older joeys are ever neglected by their mothers, even though they are excluded from the pouch when they reach an age of approximately eight months. Although their days of free transport are over, each will get his regular groomings and will also be allowed to put his head into the pouch to be suckled whenever he feels the need. If, by some mischance, a well-grown joey were to be permitted to reenter the pouch, his relatively large bulk would undoubtedly smother or crush his Lilliputian successor. During the next few months the blue flyer will be supplying her young with two different kinds of milk. Her older joey will be fed a rich, thick milk from the teat he has been using since his birth, and which is now greatly elongated, while the newcomer will be living on a clear, thin fluid ideally suited to its extreme infancy.

The oldest of the blue flyers in Wangarie's group mated, as is customary, after the birth of her last joey, and the development of the resultant dormant blastocyst was resumed seven months later when the sucking stimulus of the joey in her pouch slackened. The delayed embryo had been growing for only twenty-one days when her joey was killed by dogs, however, so her pouch has been empty for the ten days required to complete the developmental period of thirty-one days.

She is due to give birth today, on this parched morning, in the middle of a brown and dusty plain, swept by a wind out of the west and under a sun whose rays can bite like acid. On a day like this the journey soon to be attempted will be particularly hazardous, as any deviation from the shortest route from the protection of the uterus to the protection of the pouch will mean increased exposure to the dehydrating air of drought. At present, it does not seem possible that so small a traveler could long withstand the searing gusts eddying around the trees of the sand ridge.

For the next three hours the blue flyer wanders restlessly about the area, often stopping to dampen her flanks and forearms with saliva, to clean the inside of her already spotless pouch, and to lick the region of her urogenital opening. Then, at nearly ten o'clock in the morning, at the start of the hottest third of the day, she again assumes the birth position, tail stretched out between her legs and her back supported against a tree.

The wind whips up the sand from the ridge, blasts through the casuarinas, and flexes the trunks of the cypress pines. Even those kangaroos not asleep have their eyes closed. Sometimes one will move to the shelter of another tree or bush, creeping miserably to a new place while the gusts cut deep ruffs in his fur. The gray foresters, shaggier than the reds, always look the more wind-blown and bewildered.

The birth, once started, is soon over. A small quantity of fluid from the urogenital opening of the blue flyer precedes the ejection of a translucent envelope containing the waste products of the foetus. This is soon followed by the embryonic form of a kangaroo in a second translucent envelope. It quickly breaks free.

The glistening wet neonate is scarcely two centimeters long and mainly head and forelimbs. Without pausing to adjust to the violent change in the nature of the medium surrounding it and assailed by a scorching wind, the tiny creature starts to climb the wall of fur. It hauls itself vigorously upward.

Possessing that kind of semi-transparency that allows muscles and blood vessels to be seen under the skin, the miniature, although unformed, kangaroo has the appearance of a crystal model specially prepared to demonstrate the inside arrangements of an animal. Although its only means of locomotion are its disproportionately large forelimbs, the animated mite makes unerringly for the pouch. It is as well that it does so. Presumably its senses of smell and balance are working. If that is so, its sense of smell must be under stress in the windy conditions. Perhaps the journey would have ended differently if the doe, worn out by hours of waiting, had slumped sideways.

Below the new joey's open nostrils there is another hole where the mouth will later take shape, but the ears and eyes are sealed. Otherwise the rest of the creature, including what will eventually become its distinctive and, indeed, unique characteristics—its great hind limbs and tail—is merely an odd-looking bud, which its bloated forelimbs are dragging as a hermit crab drags its shell. Needle-fine claws reach the pouch as a fiercer gust of wind browns out the tossing trees, and by the time the air has cleared again the traveler has disappeared. In darkness and humidity it then attaches itself to one of the three teats that have not been enlarged by the use of the previous occupant. The particular nipple chosen will swell in the joey's mouth so that the two cannot be readily parted, except by force— and if force should be used the death of the young one from shock and loss of blood will quickly follow.

At present the chances of this paltry token of a kangaroo ever attaining maturity look pretty slim, although it will doubtless flourish while its needs remain trifling. Certainly it has been no great drain so far on the strength of a parent thirty-five thousand times heavier. It was, in fact, the extreme smallness of the kangaroo that led early Australians to believe that the joey grew out of the doe's teat like a bud. When they were first made, reports that the baby kangaroo had climbed up its parent's belly fur and attached itself to a teat in the pouch were ridiculed.

For the next month or two the newcomer will be sustained by minute quantities of a thin, clear fluid supplied from the teat to which it is attached, but a crisis could come later when a larger volume of richer milk will be required. In fact, crises can come at any time. There could have been a crisis now for her previous joey, if he had survived, for he still would have been requiring milk from the teat he had been using and, considering the continuing scarcity of green feed, it is doubtful that he would have gotten it—or, if he had been at least partly successful, whether the supply of milder fluid to the youngling attached to another of her teats would have been affected.

Soon after the birth of her latest offspring the blue flyer hops away in search of better protection from the wind, and after she has settled down no kangaroo moves for hours. For once the flies do not trouble them and there is no need for any dust to be tossed into the air. There is plenty of it whirling skyward already, although the old boomer dozing under his tree out on the plain is visible more often than he is blotted out.

Wangarie sits up late in the afternoon and, leaning forward, licks the head and the long ears of her pouched joey. So far, he has not received much attention from her. However, now that he is furred, although sparsely, and is occasionally putting his head out of the pouch, she spends more time in grooming him, often to the accompaniment of soft, sucking noises. The wind abates as the sun sinks toward the horizon and the western sky turns red, shading to pale, misty gold overhead.

Clouds temper the heat of the sun in the morning, and there is a disturbance among the kangaroos as some of them make off across the plain. Rain has been falling somewhere ahead of them. Wangarie and the other two blue flyers—and, of course, their young-at-heel—are among the pathfinders. After a while the boomer, too, gets to his feet, pauses to rasp at his ribs, then thumps heavily in their wake.

He is thirsty, they are all thirsty, and progress is steady. Other kangaroos are moving in the same direction. A three-wire fence is met with. The young ones fall through easily but there is a casualty—a big buck who essays the jump but fails and is held suspended, his hind legs having passed under the top wire and over the next. He can do nothing but scratch endlessly at the ground to the creak and sway of the wires that have trapped him. He will not live through the next day, and the grooves dug by his front claws will tell of his sufferings.

The earth tank that lies roughly across their path is not far from a homestead, and the kangaroos approach it fearfully. No sheep are now using the tank, the paddock having been cleared of stock. The night is very dark and rain is starting to fall again as the kangaroos nose up the earth bank and creep down to the muddy pool. Their hind feet squelch in the pool's edges but, otherwise, the visitors are silent. Rain patters hollowly on the water's surface. When the animals have drunk they return to the top of the bank and continue their journey. So far they have traveled only about eight kilometers because of their unremitting search for a straw or two of feed.

It is another day before they reach a place where grass has sprouted after a storm. A mob of red kangaroos is already feeding in the open, and there are perhaps two hundred gray foresters in the edges of an expanse of scrub.

Rain starts to fall again as the sun is setting. Kangaroos,

red and gray, have been arriving all afternoon and they are
still converging on the paddock when darkness falls. About
an hour later the drone of a motor becomes audible, and
some of the foresters head toward the trees. But none of
them hops very far before sitting up and staring back.
Others do not even look up. The sound of the motor
gets louder and the vehicle's lights grow sharper.

If it had been daylight or bright moonlight the mobs
would have scattered in all directions, but darkness to
them means concealment. Headlights sweep the plain as
the truck turns, and the kangaroos stir like bushes in the
wind. They sit up and watch, motionless as cardboard cut-
outs. Suddenly it is pitch dark again.

Men's voices, rattlings, and the glow of a flashlight
come from the direction of the truck, but the mob does
not take fright. However, there is now an unoccupied
space of seventy to eighty meters' radius around the source
of light and noise. Rain bedews the new grass and animals
alike. Even the clang of lifting gear falling into place fails
to startle the kangaroos. Neither the driver of the truck nor
his assistant ever looks directly at their quarry, so it is obvious that the intruders cannot see in the dark. Sometimes a
kangaroo will stare at the men and then, almost always,
resume feeding.

Quiet, except for low-toned conversation from the
truck. After a while, silence, utter silence; and, in the
silence, the blaze of a hundred-watt light. Fifty kangaroos
sit bolt upright.

Ten shots are fired before any kangaroo so much as
moves. When at last they begin to make off, blindly, toward the darkness, there are fifteen bodies on the ground,

including those of the red boomer and the blue flyer who lost her joey to the dogs. Every bullet, and they all have been fired at ranges of between one hundred and one hundred fifty meters, has hit the victim in the chest, causing death instantly or in seconds.

Dazed by glare and the crash of rifles, Wangarie, like many near her, hops a short way then looks back. Primly erect, front paws tucked in, she stares into the brain-numbing brilliance. She does this over and over again until she reaches the penumbra at the edge of the dark, when she bounds away with a greater degree of certainty. When the spotlight swings, the plains writhe with shadows. So, yet again, she stops, this time to watch the shadows fleeing as the truck roars slowly closer. But the shape of the lone blue flyer, barely discernible against the solid darkness, is not an easy mark. Besides, the rain is heavier, the truck is in its lowest gear, and no single animal—not even the biggest buck—would be worth plowing so far through the gluey soil to collect. A wide traverse of the spotlight's beam confirms the fact that there are no other kangaroos to be seen, and the light flicks off.

The assault for that night is over. The reports of a few more shots slap against Wangarie's sensitive eardrums as the truck returns to pick up the bodies and the shooters kill an occasional wounded straggler trying to escape. The dead kangaroos are gutted, butchered, and their carcasses loaded on the truck, which is cutting deeper furrows as its load increases.

Amazingly, Wangarie and most of the other kangaroos, with the exception of those who set off into the distance at the first shots, do not go very far before they are feeding as quietly as ever. The headlights of the truck are plainly visible to them as are the men's flashlights searching for bodies. When the truck wallows back on the road it is carrying twenty-eight carcasses—a poor tally for a night's work.

Sunrise over the plains the next day is spectacular. Dust from farther west where the drought has not yet broken hangs in a cloudless sky, and the sun is like polished copper. Design for morning is a red disc over a horizontal line. The red kangaroos push their long shadows before them as they leave the plain for the shelter of the trees of a sand ridge. The day will be hot. It is hot already, and exertion must be kept to a minimum. As the sun climbs, the kangaroos creep under bushes and small trees. Wangarie is lying under an ironwood, and when at length her joey emerges from her pouch he loses his balance and falls over. The sandy soil being comfortable, he stays there. Wangarie licks his forehead and ears. It is mid-February and Merloo has increased his birth weight in twenty-six weeks from .9 gram to nearly two kilograms. Nevertheless, he is no bigger than a largish rabbit, and his growth will have to continue apace for the next few weeks. The nature of the milk required by him must change, too, and it is fortunate that the last fall of rain came in time to bring on enough green feed to enable Wangarie to increase and enrich her supply.

Merloo is already beginning to nibble grass occasionally, and in another three weeks or so his weaning will have reached the stage where the sucking stimulus on the teat will have been reduced sufficiently to start the further development of the blastocyst lying dormant in Wangarie's second uterus. Thirty-one days later, when the blastocyst will have grown into a foetus ready to be delivered, Merloo will be permanently excluded from the pouch.

Mother and son doze intermittently but no lengthy period of untroubled rest is possible, yesterday's rain and today's sun having hatched hordes of stinging insects. All the kangaroos are twitching and squirming under the attacks. They shake their heads incessantly and paw and bite at their flanks and ribs.

Protected in some measure by Wangarie's constant grooming, the joey remains where he is for a while, but suddenly dives into his mother's pouch for cover. His tail and hind legs are visible for a minute or so, then another sting causes him to disappear altogether.

A multitude of birds discover the dead kangaroos' remains. Most of the scavengers are ravens, who interrupt their own conversational cawings and croakings at intervals with a peculiar low moaning that towers unexpectedly into a husky scream of amazing power and duration. Not that any of these things seem to have the slightest effect on the passivity of the kangaroos, neither the cries of the ravens nor the squealing notes of the fork-tailed kites, nor the growing stench of offal left from the butchering of their kinsmen.

Only four of the original group of seven mobile animals are left—Wangarie, the youngish mature buck, and the young blue flyer with a son-at-heel. Wangarie's young daughter, who was again separated from her mother on the same night that the boomer and the oldish blue flyer were shot, is now so far away that a reunion would be a miraculous coincidence, especially since neither will try to seek out the other. The young doe no longer needs any parental care and will probably follow another group just as contentedly as she followed Wangarie.

During this quiet spell some of the kangaroos visit an earth tank. Others do not bother since they are obtaining enough moisture from the green pick, but by the morning of the fourth day the sun and wind have so dried the earth that the kangaroos are again able to throw dust into the air to protect themselves from the flies and other insects.

Wangarie's joey frequently emerges from the pouch to make wavering journeys about the sand ridge, excursions that often end in a frantic dash for safety as the shadow of a raven or kite drifts across his path. Generally, though, he is content to sprawl close to his parent's side, where every now and then a shower of dirt lands on him. After a vigorous shaking of his head he always settles down again. Wangarie dozes, then wakes to groom him and to scoop up some more dust, dozes off, wakes to brush leaves from his back with her forepaw and to lick dust from his head and ears. She makes quiet, clucking noises and then goes to sleep again. A gray forester buck, restlessly changing from one place to another, bumps into her in passing and the joey vanishes into her pouch.

That night, at dusk, the sound of the heavy truck is heard again as the shooters for the pet food and furred skin markets continue their operations. Some of the kangaroos move off at once, their dim shapes showing against the eastern sky where it is brightening above the black wall of the horizon. Before the moon's rim appears, a spotlight is switched on.

Having dry ground under it, the truck is able to get

quite close to the mob, and dazed kangaroos sitting up like targets in a shooting gallery hurl themselves down to a series of explosions so loud that they seem to numb those not already dead. Stopping only to pick the larger animals out of each group, the truck drones steadily on. Most are killed outright, and any kangaroo seen struggling is dispatched, shockingly but swiftly, by a single, beheading blow of a broad-bladed tomahawk.

Although twice caught in the spotlight, Wangarie is too far away—about three hundred meters—for accurate shooting. Besides, there are plenty of easier marks.

Swiftly now, the moon rises. It is a full moon and the behavior of the quarry changes as the mysterious silver flood pours down upon the grasslands. Those kangaroos caught in the spotlight remain as motionless as before, but those farther out disappear into the distance.

Wangarie and the other three of her group are already out of range. Behind them a few more shots echo across the plain, then there is silence as the men put their rifles away and prepare for the next phase of their work—a grisly business carried out with knife and tomahawk, as bloody as in any abattoir. Only the carcass, gutted and trimmed but not skinned, will be accepted at the freezing works; heads, entrails, feet, and tails are of no interest and are usually left for the foxes and birds of prey.

However, the two shooters are not carrying out a completely routine operation because they have a government order for skulls of every size from that of a small joey's upwards. Therefore the heads of all the kangaroos killed are gathered up and tossed into an empty drum, which was bouncing around in the back of the truck on the outward journey but is now stable by reason of the weight in it and the carcasses piled around it.

Splashed with blood from the butchering, and perspiring, the men are constantly troubled by the fur that floats around them like vapor. As they work on in the light of a kerosene lamp they keep wiping their hands on their overalls and rubbing their faces into the crooks of their arms to rid themselves of the tormenting filaments sticking to skin, eyelashes, and brows. They are soaked in sweat as the last carcass—that of a big buck—is swung to the top of the load. When he has checked the gear and stowed it aboard, the owner of the outfit takes a rag from under the front seat and rubs his hands. His offsider, or helper, also cleans away the worst of the blood and turns out the light.

The motor rumbles, the tires jerk out of the depressions they have made in the soft soil, and the heaps of entrails, feet, and tails glide out of the side glow of the headlights. The heavily laden truck roars and sideslips diagonally up the low earth embankment to the formed road.

It is an hour's run into town, and for most of the way there is a conversational void inside the cabin. But there is tobacco smoke, and every so often a match flares. The driver is thinking about the secondary contract he has signed for the supply of kangaroo heads. He almost wishes he had turned it down because, tomorrow, when he takes the drum of heads to the Wildlife Research people, he will be asked when he intends to correct the imbalance in the ages of the specimens delivered.

He thought he would get extra income by simply bringing back the heads of animals shot for the freezing works but, unfortunately, the department requires a full range, from the time the first tooth pushes through the gum to the time the last falls out from old age.

It is known that the teeth of kangaroos are subject to a singular development—the gradual progression of the grinding teeth along the jawbone as the animal gets older—and that the rate of this progression, together with other factors, provides a reliable means of reckoning a kangaroo's age. The movement does not apply to the incisors, although they are of special interest, too, in their own way. There are three pairs of incisors in the top jaw and one pair in the lower. The upper incisors are as firmly based as those of other animals, but when the kangaroo is grazing, the lower pair operates with a slight shearing action made possible by the division of the lower jawbone and the elasticity of the tissue linking the two halves. Although slight, this spread enables the kangaroo to gather in extra grass with every "mouthful." But the incisors are not part of the process to be charted as a means of assessing age. It is the molars and premolars that reveal this information.

The first grinding teeth to appear in the mouth of a young kangaroo are two premolars and a molar, these three generally being well established by the time the joey is four months out of the pouch. It is about then—a year after its birth—that the red kangaroo is refused further milk from its mother and must rely on grass and, to a lesser extent, the leaves of certain trees and shrubs to keep itself alive.

The next tooth to appear, another molar, comes through the jawbone at the end of the row of three, which have moved forward to make room for it. Now the row has four teeth, two premolars and two molars. During the forward movement of the existing teeth and the arrival and growth of the next two molars, both of the first premolars are dislodged in favor of a single, or "permanent," premolar, which is also shed in its turn—pushed over the edge, so to speak, by the continuing advance of the molars, now four in number.

Even then the progression does not stop, although it does slow down. The actual rate of deceleration has not been worked out yet. It is possible, although very unusual, for a kangaroo to live on until most of its teeth have completed their journey along the jawbone and fallen out and the odd one or two left are so worn as to be useless. With no means of mastication the animal soon starves to death.

When all the information from a complete range of skulls has been collected and tabulated, scientists and students will have a method of telling the age of kangaroos that will be far in advance of any other and almost as effective in the field as in the laboratory.

Methods such as weighing and measuring the total animal are only rough guides at best because the data vary so widely according to the health of the subject. Assessing a kangaroo's age by inspecting the amount of wear on its teeth is likewise a pretty approximate business. The differences between kangaroos living in contrasting habitats can be very great. Some are born into an environment where seasons are generally good and feed is plentiful. The grass there, besides being green, is washed periodically by the rain. Others may have to battle it out where food is always scarce and the wind makes sure that everything has its film of dust.

So the rangier, leaner kangaroos of the desert fringe may have their molars ground down almost to the gums from the dust they take in with every snip of grass or old man salt bush while the teeth of their kinsmen of similar age but living farther east may show comparatively little wear.

The strength of the new system lies in the fact that the teeth of any two kangaroos of the same age will always be identical in number and type and in their positions in the jawbone in relation to a fixed point in the skull. The forward progression of kangaroos' teeth, even to the slowing down of the forward movement in later years, follows the same pattern in every animal.   1982363

Although the driver may not be aware of every one of the reasons why the heads he is collecting must be representative of the whole life of the kangaroo as it is affected by the growth and eventual deterioration of its teeth, he does realize that he will now have to make a special effort to kill some animals with carcasses well below the minimum legal weight.

"So we'll have to do a bit of shooting just for the heads. That is, if we want to get paid—well, we gotta fill the contract, I suppose."

He sounds as though he is summing up after a long discussion. Which he is, in a way, the matter having been mentioned repeatedly during the last week or so.

"We'll need seventy young 'roos and some joeys to complete the sets," the driver and contractor continues as he swings the truck into the deserted main street of Cobar. The hour is three A.M.

"That's what I reckon. We can get something for their carcasses, too. We might as well dress 'em even if they are underweight."

"No, not on your life. We leave the carcasses, mate. Too many arguments. Can't you hear that inspector at the works? 'Here, what's these underweight carcasses doin' here? Yair, who says you got a permit? Where is it?' and 'Who the hell signed it? Never bloody heard of him—or the department. Besides, this permit's only for heads. Nothing on it about carcasses. Go on, get 'em out of here, pronto. Yer damn lucky I'm not gonna report you. I will, too, if you don't get outa me sight.' No, we won't be touchin' no underweight carcasses. Not if we had fifty special permits for heads. We leave 'em to the crows."

"Okay, okay, I only mentioned it."

All permits, which are issued by the National Parks and Wildlife Service, control the killing of kangaroos in areas where shooting is legal by setting minimum weights for dressed carcasses. These weights may vary according to the level of the kangaroo population but are usually about twelve kilograms for gray foresters and twenty kilograms for red kangaroos, allowing more latitude in the taking of gray foresters, which are more numerous than reds in many regions. The minimum weight of twenty kilograms for a red kangaroo means that only full-grown bucks and the largest blue flyers may be shot with safety. The average-size blue flyer would not weigh twenty kilograms as a trimmed carcass.

Accordingly, the killing of small kangaroos is regarded as a waste of ammunition by the professional carcass hunter, and any shot by mistake are left where they lie.

Permits issued for the destruction of kangaroos in localities where they have reached pest proportions do not carry any restriction on the size or age of the animals shot.

The truck stops in the yard of the freezing works and the men start to transfer the carcasses to a cool-room for official scrutiny when the inspector arrives.

March

THE DROUGHT-BREAKING RAINS have fallen, and stopped and fallen again without any deluges or cloudbursts. So there are no muddy currents to swirl around bridges and no stagnant lakes stretching as far as the eye can see.

Instead, the plains already have a pale green tint. Their color becomes more definite as further showers and intervals of sunshine follow, and soon the grass will be tall enough to be ruffled like the sea when the wind blows.

With so large a part of the eastern edge of the plains being turned into plowed fields, the red kangaroos are moving deeper into the sheep country.

That is the way Wangarie is going, and her journey has no migratory urge. Forced east of her known range by drought, she is now returning to the wider land. No doubt her recent experiences in the more closely settled areas— too many shooters operating by spotlight, too many fences, and too many dogs that bark from lighted home- steads—have had their effect also; but, in the main, she is following the spread of the new grass westward.

At the beginning of March she is near Coonamble, on the banks of the Castlereagh. The Walgett road is so close that sometimes the flash of a windshield in the sun may be seen as a momentary pinpoint of light in the distance. It is the middle of the afternoon, and flocks of galahs in the river red gums, having taken their siesta during the hottest part of the day, are coming to life again. They do not come to life quietly. Some march along the great branches, raising their crests and screeching. Others balance on the highest twigs or take short display flights as though to show off the undersurfaces of their wings which are as pink as their breasts.

Wangarie is the picture of tranquility. A hot wind is soughing through the river oaks and the blue flyer is resting in her favorite position, propped on an elbow. Her head is drooping and her eyes are closed but her ears are alert; they flick and turn occasionally. Her free forepaw has scraped a curve in the black soil about the size and shape of a boomerang and, every now and then, she sprinkles dust, the flies being troublesome in spite of the wind. They come in under the lee of her body to sting her and the joey lying beside her, mercilessly.

Merloo, like most very young bucks, is a mixture of the two distinguishing colors of his species. He is bluish red on the back, shading to purple on the forehead and neck and at the butt of the tail. Nearly two weeks of March have gone by and, at seven and a half months, he is partly weaned. If the decrease in the stimulation of the teat he has been using has conveyed its proper message, the waiting blastocyst will already be in the middle of its gestation period, and Wangarie's next offspring should be born in fifteen or sixteen days. When that happens Merloo will have to keep up with his mother under his own power and, if pursued, he will have to rely on his own speed.

At present he looks too big to fit into the pouch. However, much of the instability that plagued him earlier has been overcome, and he makes an excursion to nibble a tuft of grass without a stumble. The length of the grass stems is appreciably reduced before the return journey.

The other flyer in the group is sheltering behind a cluster of river oak saplings that bend over her when the wind hisses through their needlelike branchlets. The wind has not stopped since dawn. Her young-at-heel is sprawled in the same patch of shade, his pale and slender hind limbs still unproven. He is a lanky creature, not robust but pretty fast when it comes to flight. He is rather more than sixteen months old, but the drought has set back his development and it will be at least another year before he matures.

Later in the afternoon the only full-grown buck in the company starts down the river bank to drink, and the river is mostly a river of sand rippled and contoured by the flow of the current from the last rains. Quiet pools reflect the branches of the river red gums and there are hollows where the stream has eddied.

It is cooler between the winding, earthen ramparts, and the red buck takes his time. He makes deep prints in the sand as he creeps along and, all the time, especially while he drinks, he is watched, suspiciously, by the flocks of pink and gray galahs. They are not uneasy, simply critical. They mutter among themselves, hoping to find fault. Sidling down a fallen branch, a line of them waits for the gigantic creature to go. As he turns he strikes the end of the branch with his foot and, instantly, every bird on it utters a piercing scream and takes to the air. Those in the

trees overhead do likewise, whole flocks circling up deaf-
eningly and spectacularly into the cloudless sky.

Climbing back up the river's terraced flood banks, the
cause of the commotion finally reaches the top—and looks
straight into the eyes of a stranger of impressive stature and
unfriendly mien. The fact that the stranger is an enlarged
replica of himself does not make him any more welcome.
None of the others, except Merloo, has so far taken any
notice of the newcomer. Merloo is thunderstruck. He is
sitting bolt upright with his small back recurved and his
forepaws drooping.

After they have stared at one another the buck who has
just returned from the pool in the river bed decides to go
farther along the bank before making his final bound to
the level of the plains. The stranger remains vigilant. The
powdery substance encrimsoning his throat and upper
chest, which is said to be a glandular exudation to attract
the female, also adds greatly to his threat display as he
rears up to his full height to balance on his toes and the
end of his tail. He towers over the other. Hollowing his
back and stretching sideways with his neck extended and
his head pointing downwards, he saws at his ribs with the
sharp claws of a spread forepaw. It is a strange gesture, neither provocative nor conciliatory, and its rasping noise is
distinct in the quiet moments between the screams of the
galahs again settling into the tops of the river red gums.
The younger buck turns aside to crop a brown and dusty
tussock that, to any herbivore with a liking for the succu-
lence of short, green grass, must be about as appetizing as
the bristles of an upturned scrubbing brush.

As the latest addition to the group—and, apparently,
that is what he is—falls to licking his forearms, the sinking

sun throws into relief the veins, muscles, and sinews of his powerful, rather gaunt, body and lights up the rose bloom of his throat and upper chest, that rich powdering which can be brushed away in life and which fades so quickly in death. He, too, noses at the ground, sighs, and, collapsing with an audible thump, rolls over on his back like a horse in a sand pit. The sun having lost its heat, he remains there awhile enjoying the warmth of the ground before he turns onto his side and props himself on his elbow, lounging and yawningly squinting into the fiery west. His head, his distinctive ears, blunt muzzle, and the line of his profile curving down to nose and mouth are decidedly equine; the conspicuous black whisker marks set off by the whitish lower part of his face add further interest to the picture of a big buck kangaroo luxuriously drowsing in the dust—a typical old man red.

Leaving the trees together, the galahs circle over the plains, the flock turning so exactly in unison that the cloud of soft grayness is changed instantly to pink then, as they continue to swing, to gray again. They flutter down into the grass. Although the sky is bright with sunlight the red kangaroos start getting to their feet. Merloo makes a dive for his mother's pouch and, aided by her forward crouching position, scrambles in, turns the usual somersault, and thrusts out his head. He is a weighty burden, distending the blue flyer's pouch to its full extent. Old Man Red is the last to rouse and the last to go slidingly down the bank into the shadows now filling the narrow ravine of the Castlereagh. Gleaming like black glass, a pool in a depression scooped out by an eddy tells the passer-by how deep he must dig into the sand if he would drink in some other part of the river bed; dead branches and nests of debris caught in the trees show the flood heights of past years.

As the kangaroos emerge onto the plains a small black-and-white bird half flies, half runs along the bank, rises vertically to take an insect, then glides to the ground to swing its tail—and, to only a slightly lesser degree, itself—from side to side in the lively manner of its kind, at the same time uttering a string of melodious and cheerful-sounding notes. A similar call comes from nearby and another, similar, bird appears, the two joining in a chase as light and pert as the flight of butterflies.

While searching through the long grass for a place where sheep have fed and where there may be a regrowth of shorter, sweeter grass, the kangaroos are followed by the willy-wagtails, the sun shining through their wings as they loop and dive around them and sometimes settle on their backs. A part of the plain itself seems to take flight as the galahs rise under the kangaroos' noses to flare into pink brilliance when they wheel toward the river. The flock is swallowed up, screaming, by the trees on the river bank. Not so much because the sun is about to set but because the chance of being caught in open country by a bird of prey is becoming dangerously real the farther they venture from cover, the willy-wagtails fly back to the river.

Soon, the kangaroos are only shapes in the gloom of dusk, and there is no sound but the breeze in the grass. They move slowly and stop often, once for an hour where the feed is good. Merloo is leaning so far out of Wangarie's pouch that his small forepaws, firmly on the ground, are able to walk when she edges forward. He, too, is grazing and, after a while, he leaves the pouch altogether. He is bolder under cover of darkness.

The younger of the two bucks affects to take no notice of his new and magnificent rival. In fact, neither seems conscious of the other's presence, and there is certainly room for them both under the stars. The plains are darkness and stars.

Later, much later, a light sparkles on the Coonamble to Walgett road, and when the light and the distant sound of a motor fade, the silence seems the more intense because of the faraway barking of a fox. Only a couple of hours remain until dawn when the red kangaroos lie down to rest. They have crawled through a badly rusted panel of a wire-netted fence and fed to satiety on moisture-loving herbs and succulents growing where the run-off from the highway and the hot, sunny weather have provided ideal conditions. No traffic has passed since they have been there, and when headlights do appear they flicker like danger signals through far-off clumps of trees. Then the big motor transport, having worked up a great speed over many kilometers of empty, level highway, is on them and past them in a stunning explosion of noise and glare.

Now that the danger is a diminishing rumble in the dark, all the kangaroos, with the single exception of Merloo, bounce to a stop and sit up in attenuated attitudes of alarm. They are all staring in the same direction. None of them has been hit.

Slowly picking himself up after a collision with a fence post, Merloo creeps dazedly along the line of the netting while Wangarie and the younger blue flyer, her joey close at heel, make anxiously toward him, both irresistibly drawn by his cries of distress. In response to their soft cluckings he keeps pushing against the mysterious barrier that looks so frail and is yet so strong. It seems to go on forever and then, suddenly, he is through or, rather, over—a fallen white cypress pine having flattened a panel of netting.

Wangarie holds him with her forepaws while she nuzzles him to make sure he is hers then, letting him into her pouch, turns and hops heavily away. One by one the motionless figures around her come alive and follow. The fence wires twang as the younger buck sprawls through—the older, bigger buck is already well ahead, having cleared the obstacle without seeing it, in the earlier panic.

Of all the members of the company, Merloo, in one respect at least, is the most fortunate. Kangaroos, being slightly built above the haunches, are particularly susceptible to injuries to the forelimbs, neck, ribs, and shoulders from collisions, and many a full-grown buck has been killed in this manner. A kangaroo the size of Merloo damages only himself, but a big animal, dazzled, terrified, and at full speed, is a danger both to himself and, worse, to the driver of the vehicle coming toward him.

The red kangaroos head in the direction of the Macquarie Marshes. They have a long way to go when two more strangers—a blue flyer with a young doe-at-heel—emerge from a creek bed and trail after them. Streaked with washaways and gutters, the terrain thereabouts is a miniature badlands. Sharp-edged channels wind like black rivers through the dawn and, where they divide, buttes of eroded earth are turning red in the strengthening light of day.

Having crossed a series of dry watercourses, the kangaroos cast about for shelter and are soon widely dispersed under the drooping canes of a few lignum bushes. Wangarie, Merloo, and Old Man Red share the shade of the only tree—a leopard wood—and the feet and tail of the buck are in the sun.

The day is already hot. Gusts of wind are lifting the dust from the claypans and rippling the silvery grasses; the kestrel hovering against the sky sweeps away in a long, descending curve to alight on a lignum cane but is unable to maintain his balance, although his russet wings beat frantically.

Wangarie has been at rest for about an hour when the young Merloo leaves her pouch and hops out into the sun. The blue flyer lifts her head to watch him and makes soft sounds. He hops farther away, but the sun is too hot so he returns to the shade. The wind stirs his reddish blue fur. Getting to her feet, Wangarie grooms him carefully with her front paws—carefully, because her claws are long and sharp. Then she licks him from head to foot. When Merloo tries to get back into her pouch he is stopped. He tries again and is again fended off, quietly but decidedly. Since the blue flyer's forward crouching position is inviting, a brief scuffle ensues, but the young one can make no headway. However, Wangarie consents to suckle him, so he drags her pouch open and there is quiet for a while. Then, as though hoping to take her by surprise, he makes an even more determined attempt to gain entrance. But he is pushed away, and when Wangarie lies down he lies down beside her. He has become a young-at-heel.

It is late afternoon, and the kestrel is again hunting the grasslands when the kangaroos start to graze. Wangarie is slow to quit the shelter of the lignum. The wind makes no difference to her progress, but it often blows Merloo temporarily off course.

April

THOSE SEARING DAYS of summer that so often find their way into autumn have run out early this year, and the weather, although hot at noon, has been pleasantly warm for the most part. Accordingly, the red kangaroos are no longer mainly nocturnal. For some time now they have been feeding when they are hungry, day or night, and resting when they are not hungry. Mornings and afternoons are generally spent grazing or basking, and it is only when the sun is high that they seek the shade.

The dispersal of the big mobs is continuing as grass becomes more plentiful, and Wangarie's group has not seen any other kangaroos for some days. Even the group itself has spread out. Now that the Castlereagh, with its river red gums and the westernmost of the plains' river oaks, has been left behind and the red kangaroos are well toward the center of a black soil plain, there are few evidences of other life of any kind. Occasionally a flock of galahs flies

over, and early one morning fifteen emus emerge in a
line, it seems, out of the ground. Quickly losing the formation forced on them by the narrowness of the water-
course they have just crossed, they stalk about the plain
with high, slow-motion steps, snapping up seeds and
grasses. Although none of them ever looks at the
kangaroos, they feed near them for a while before pecking
their way on into the distance.

Since excluding Merloo from her pouch on the last day
of March—and the development of her blastocyst being
strictly on time—Wangarie has been cleaning her pouch
for the reception of its next occupant. Making its preliminary entrance into the world on the following afternoon,
the young kangaroo climbs the fur of the blue flyer's belly
and disappears again a few minutes later into the safety of
her pouch. There it quickly noses out one of the three
small teats. The fourth, which is still being used by Merloo, is too greatly enlarged to be encompassed by the
mouth of the new arrival.

No sooner has the newborn joey attached itself than the
end of the teat starts to swell and it is not long before the
usual marsupial ball-and-socket connection has been ef-
fected. So, in the humid dark, it hangs there, smaller than
a sparrow's egg and weighing about the same. It will not be
noticed again for at least three months, either as a burden
or as a drain upon the blue doe's ability to supply it with
milk. Its widely open nostrils and disproportionately large
forelimbs with their needle-fine claws have played their
parts in getting it this far, and it is now the responsibility of
the mouth to maintain its grip and supply the rest of the

body with enough nourishment for its development from a blind bud to a full-grown kangaroo.

A few hours after the birth Wangarie sets out for an earth tank about two kilometers across the plain. It is not often in this cooler weather that she bothers to drink, and she is in no hurry. Her pace varies from her slowest, when she often uses her tail to support her while she searches through the grass stems for green shoots, to the more characteristic gait of the kangaroo as she hops slowly across a claypan. Merloo is able to keep up without difficulty. Going there, including a number of stops and frequent changes of course, takes an hour and a half, and when she and her gangling young-at-heel are descending the sloping side of the tank the sun is well down toward the horizon. A coterie of galahs, their pinkness reflected in the water, are drinking together from the muddy edges, and a gray teal is preening its feathers on the sunny eastern slope where the black soil is dry and cracked.

Suddenly, the younger of the two bucks of the group appears over the mound around the tank. He drinks alongside the blue flyer, and when she leaves he goes with her. The plains are very quiet, and as the kangaroos return toward their feeding place there is only the swish of their feet through the grass and the muted thud of pads when they chance to land on bare earth. The pace is faster now, and Merloo's shorter legs are pumping hard. The buck keeps crowding the doe. When he tries to grasp her she utters an angry cry and strikes at him, ripping a puff of fur out of the side of his neck. This unexpected flurry so startles Merloo that he veers off on a different course and

then, a few moments later, comes back in such a headlong
rush that it is only by sheer agility that Wangarie keeps
from trampling him. She is very quick. She could have
leaped clean over his head when he was at the top of his
flight if such an action had become necessary to avoid a
collision. Spindly shadows in the grass make strange play
as they go. The only one of the group to react to their
approach is the old man red, and he stands up to his full
height. Wangarie and Merloo swing to the side but the
young buck confronts the old man red. Although some six
or seven meters apart, they make grabs at one another with
their taloned forepaws and bare their teeth.

The display continues. Each tries to overtop the other, a
duel that shows the older to be the taller. They arch their
backs and rasp their claws across their ribs. They utter
weird, strangled noises, growlings and harsh coughings.
They bite the fur of their chests and shake as with rage.
Both are salivating copiously. Then, unexpectedly, there is
a lull in their threatenings while they lick their forearms.

But the interval does not last, and it is only minutes
before they drop down on all fours and, shuddering vio-
lently from the stress that is tensing every sinew, creep
toward each other. Having tried to make themselves taller
than life they now try to make themselves wider by jutting
out their elbows and spreading their hind legs. Saliva is
running from their mouths in glistening, long-sliding
streams. They look like two great terrestrial crabs.

Rising simultaneously to their toes and the end of their
tails, they come to close quarters in a series of short, danc-
ing hops, clutching and striking savagely at one another,
each with his head held so far back to avoid the risk of a

slashed throat that it is a wonder he can see his opponent at all. Ears laid back like those of angry dogs, they collide, the two kangaroos are chest to chest, and the aspect of the fight now seems to prove that herbivores, once roused, yield nothing in ferocity to flesh-eaters. Their cries become louder and fiercer, their gaspings more stertorous; their hind feet slip on the grass and the younger buck rips a bloody furrow across the challenger's muzzle.

Even so, he is being overpowered. Long, sinewy arms thrusting at his neck at last, inevitably, obtain the hold that enables the taller animal to steady himself and, balancing momentarily on his tail, to kick out with all the power of his hind legs. The twin blows hurl the other backwards and he crashes to the ground. He is up on all fours in an instant, dazed but not badly injured. But there is no fight left in him so he turns submissively away, nose to ground as though feeding. Fortunately for him the double blow had been delivered from a cramped position because the fighters were so closely locked together, more like an almighty shove than the fearful slash it might have been if either of the chisellike nails on the victor's hind feet had penetrated the skin.

Without attempting to follow up his advantage, Old Man Red turns his attention to Wangarie. Her last blastocyst having been developed and finally born, she is now ready to accept a mate and will probably remain in oestrus for another day or so. Whether or not she mates within that period, however, she will not return to the oestrous cycle until the sucking stimulus of her present youngling weakens or stops.

There are three or four occasions during her courtship

when she turns on the buck with clawings and sharp cries, but he keeps on following her and nosing her tail and cloacal eminence until at last she crouches down. He grasps her around the shoulders and they copulate for three or four minutes before the doe breaks away. The two then graze side by side until morning, when the buck goes to a sleeping place in the sun. His enemy of last night looks up as he passes by, yawns, and dozes off again.

More showers from the west make almost certain a supply of winter feed in that direction, and every time the eight kangaroos change to another paddock it is west of the last. It is as though Wangarie is reenacting in reverse her slow drift eastward of nearly a year ago, when to have remained in the same place would have meant starvation.

She is not far from the Macquarie Marshes where the rains following the dry spell have not been quite heavy enough to drown the drought-resisting lignum bushes choking the system of watercourses; the moderate flooding of the region is now subsiding. Most of the overflow has already drained away, and the marshes are again bursting with life. Falcons and eagles are hunting the wildfowl attracted to their swamps and billabongs while lesser predators await an opportunity to raid any unguarded nest. Every peninsula and cape is green with new growth, and the ground is veined with animal tracks, some of them pitted with the sharp hoofs of feral pigs.

It is an unusual kind of country, containing not only the channels of past washaways but also tracts of grassland, belts of trees, and some open forest. Like so much of inland Australia, it is subject to drought and flood with temperate intervals of uncertain duration in between and scant discernible rhythm in its fluctuations. The marshes flood, winter or summer, when the rain comes, and when the rain stops the water quickly drains away. Some marshy places always remain, however, and these are where the big rookeries of aquatic birds soon reestablish themselves—they and those that prey on them. If a drought lasts long enough even the lignum bushes may die back to their rootstocks and for a time the marshes become marshes in name only. Sun-baked mud appears where ducks and geese have swum and willy willies rattle the leaves of the trees on the ridges and whirl dust out of bare channels that were once full of water.

Although the open grassy stretches that occur in the marshes are all part of the same big plain, many of them do have the appearance of plateaus because of the extent of the erosion around them. The red kangaroos are grazing on one of these. Unlike the gray foresters, they never go into the lignum-choked watercourses except to cross to another feeding ground where, no doubt, the grass looks greener.

The evening is fine and mild. It is peaceful, too. The quacking of black ducks comes from nearby and, every now and then, a raven croaks from a cluster of trees on the far side of the lagoon.

Before it is quite dark ten or so gray foresters emerge from various paths out of the lignum and join the red kangaroos. The largest of the grays is a buck about the same size as the larger of the red bucks, although he looks

heavier because of the shagginess of his coat. More gray
foresters appear and by midnight there are thirty of them
grazing placidly under the stars. Most of the youngsters are
close to two years old or even older, as young gray foresters
remain at heel longer than red kangaroos. It is the recent
drought, of course, that has upset the age pattern of the
grays and probably accounts for the absence of any joeys
around the age of the two youngest red kangaroos. Certainly, gray foresters do have a fairly well-defined breeding
season but, in spite of this, mating will take place at other
times of the year if a gray doe should lose her young one
prematurely.

That night while the kangaroos, both gray and red,
graze and sleep, the gruntings of feral pigs in the lignum
thickets never stop, and sometimes the solid black bulk of
a boar or sow will cross the plateau to descend into the
channel on the other side. Such travelers never linger or
cast about for food but always seem intent on moving
along as quickly as possible, as though the grassland had
no attraction in comparison with the swamps and bogs surrounding it.

The fox is different. He, too, comes over the bank out
of the lignum, but silently. He is a dog fox. The young
Merloo, in one of those fits of exuberance that seize the
offspring of fleet animals, dashes around Wangarie and is
instantly followed by the female young-at-heel of his own
age, whose dam and Wangarie chance to be resting
together. The fox freezes, a front paw hanging in mid-step.
Neither joey has ventured outside a tight circle drawn
around the does, but they tire quickly. They slow down

and come to a halt and lie down again, beside their parents.

Making no attempt at concealment, unless the smoothness and directness of his approach could be construed as such, the fox runs straight at the blue flyers and their young. He makes no noise and is not seen until he is close. Even then he is not comprehended but merely glimpsed. The blue flyers do not wait. Their hind feet hit the ground in instant take-off, and two streamlined bodies arch away in different directions, bunching and bounding again. Panic! That inevitable panic, triggered by a stealthy shape in the starlight.

As for the young-at-heel, they are no longer at heel but a long way back. Nevertheless, they, too, will be saved by their fleetness. They were not as quick off the mark as the flyers, but fear has seized them, too, fear of some deadly danger, and when they do get started they look like a couple of greyhounds, they are so swift and skim so closely over the grass tops.

The fox would not have caught either in the short run. He may, possibly, have caught one eventually if a gray buck had not joined the stampede and, being immediately passed by the flyers and, moments later, by the joeys, become an involuntary rear guard. He is oldish, ponderous, of sedentary habit and inclined to truculence. So he soon slows. A solitary fox, once identified, is no more than another annoyance. So the gray buck turns around, his front claws ready to grab or slash.

Veering away, the fox pauses to sniff around some bushes, then patters off unhurriedly. In any case he has been living well lately on eggs and nestlings, with an occasional piglet, very different fare from the lean months of drought when he had been feeding on quandongs, roots, and beetles.

After a good deal of anxious searching and crying out, the two blue flyers and their joeys are reunited, and before the sun is clear of the horizon the red kangaroos have descended into the next channel to take a path zig-zagging between the lignum clumps. None of them stops to browse the new shoots as the gray foresters would have. They seem anxious to quit the close-pressing wilderness.

The next island of grassland is about the same size as the last, and the group goes no farther that day. Gray foresters dotted about this feeding ground move back toward the lignum scrub as the light strengthens. Their shaggy coats are dark with dew. A large young-at-heel looks as though he had fallen into the water. The morning light sparkles on the clear drops collecting on bedraggled tags of fur hanging from his head and neck; grass seeds fringe his eyes and are matted on his forehead. He looks shades darker than he does when dry.

Before descending into the lignum he sits there awhile in the sun and scratches himself, chest, belly, and hips. Most of the foresters tarry a little to comb their fur and to nibble at those parts of their bodies they can reach with their teeth, for, being creatures of the woodlands, forests, and scrubs, they suffer more acutely than the reds from ticks, lice, and other parasites.

One by one the gray foresters disappear until only the youngster is left. He settles down to groom himself more thoroughly. Stretched out here and there on the grassy plain, the red kangaroos are already nodding off in the sunshine. A blue flyer jumps to her feet and, followed by her plum-colored joey, hops to a bare patch of earth where she comes to rest again. When the joey lies beside her, they are almost indistinguishable from the tussocks and claypans around them. Then Merloo and Wangarie discover that they have lost one another; but they are reunited again after a repetition of squeaking calls and some agitated searching by the joey.

The young gray forester on the edge of the channel is delicately pushing a grass seed from the rim of his eye with his great hind foot. Without a doubt the talons of his front paws would be unsuited for such work—but then neither could any much clumsier device be imagined for the operation than his huge hind foot. Yet the whole limb is steady—steadier than his nervy front paws could ever be—and, in any case, it is the backs of two tiny claws that actually wipe the seed from the rim of the eye.

The precision of the performance is as extraordinary as the instrument used—the syndactylous claws, which are all that are left of two toes that have long since ceased to play any part in the carrying of the animal. During the process of their degeneration these toes have become enclosed in a single fold of skin. They are therefore twin claws, or a double claw. Now used only for grooming and for removing seeds and parasites from sensitive areas, they are carried so high on the inside of the hind feet that they never leave a track, even in soft ground.

It is the next toe, massive and elongated, that takes the

weight when the kangaroo is bounding along or standing up to its full height, although a smaller outside toe will also make a track unless the kangaroo is traveling really fast.

All kangaroos, with the exception of a single rainforest species, the musky rat kangaroo, have only four toes on the hind foot. Their degenerate, almost vestigial, twin toes are on the inside of the foot; then comes the hugely developed main toe with an auxiliary, but markedly smaller, toe on the outside. Therefore, a heavy kangaroo, whether accelerating or traveling at top speed, or weaving or dodging or sailing over a heap of fallen brushwood, exerts its thrust through two toes—one on each hind foot and called the fourth toe—and to a much smaller extent, its two humbler outside, or fifth, toes.

And the fact that the last toe of a four-toed animal may, as in this instance, be correctly described as its fifth is really perfectly straightforward, zoologically. It is not the fifth toe that is out of order. It is the first that is nonexistent. So, having discarded its first toe altogether, the kangaroo is now left with numbers two and three—the twin toes—its massive main toe, and, finally, the last of the four—which is the fifth.

Suddenly interrupting his concentration upon himself, the young kangaroo on the edge of the channel sits up and looks around. He seems to have grown larger since his grooming, and the sun and breeze have dried his fur. The day is now brilliant, and the gray forester, as though overcome by the openness of the plains and the clarity of the sky with their impression of immeasurable space—he being a creature of the forests and scrublands—turns and disappears down the slope into the lignum. Shadows flicker reassuringly across him as he noses along a narrow track to a hump of land where there are trees. Others of his kind are already there, most of them lying in patches of sunlight. It is possible to catch glimpses of blue sky on all sides, right down to ground level, but there is plenty of cover on all sides, too.

Gray foresters are very like red kangaroos in many ways. They are at once as indolent and as restless, sleeping or drowsing for long periods, then getting up to move to another spot. With the cooler weather they, too, are becoming less nocturnal and often feed in the daytime, although they seldom venture out of the trees much before dusk. They browse more than the reds and are more inclined to be content with the long, tussocky grasses that grow among trees and in poorer country, whereas the reds are always searching for the shorter grasses and green shoots. Although generally about the same size as the red kangaroos, the gray foresters look sturdier because they have longer coats and do not have the pale-colored legs that give the reds a slimmer, racier appearance. The foresters have more pointed muzzles than the reds, and the does are the same color as the bucks.

As the end of the month approaches the sky clouds over and it starts to rain. But, very soon, the overcast splits in the west, low down to the horizon, and the rift widens, turning the rain into golden mist and gilding the grass tops and the water-filmed claypans. Wangarie, who has been feeding along the edge of the last of the eroded channels, goes down the bank and along a track through the lignum. Pools have formed here and there, but the rain has stopped and the stars are out. Merloo follows the blue flyer as she pushes on, and others of the group can be heard behind them. When the red kangaroos at last reach a wide plain they are all liberally splashed with mud, Merloo and the female about his age being covered from head to toe.

Joeys-at-heel always have unhappy times when the group is forced into a "line ahead" formation, for to precede the grown kangaroos is to risk being knocked sprawling, while to follow them is to breathe dust in dry weather and to be plastered with mud in wet. But the raindrops held by the tall windmill grass of the plains wash them clean as they move on, and that night Merloo hears for the first time the wild, lost cries of the bush curlews. Later, after they have traveled farther, he hears the same weird chorus, then again—when he does not even lift his head.

For almost the whole of April the red kangaroos and the gray foresters have been living within the boundaries of the Macquarie Marshes Wildlife Reserve, where they have been protected from the professional and the amateur hunter alike. Now the small company has passed beyond the boundary line.

The plain is vast. There are no gray foresters, and they see only an occasional red, for the dispersal of the big mobs that converged on any patches of feed they could find in drought time is now complete. Nights are fine and days are warm. A raven or a hawk may cross the sky, and once a puff of dust balloons up in the distance. Otherwise, nothing. The red kangaroos stay where they are. There is food and the shelter of a few trees and bushes in case the weather should become unpleasantly hot or windy. While conditions are as they are, the kangaroos will never need to move again. But they are wayward creatures and, like humans, often do things without good reason.

May

WANGARIE, MERLOO, and a buck of eighteen months are lying under a coolabah tree.

The wind is worrying them. If they face it they must keep their heads down and their eyes narrowed, for the dust is flying, although not thickly enough to be visible except as a thin haze between them and the next lot of trees. If they turn their backs to it their fur is blown into ruffs and this disturbs them, too.

Wangarie gets to her feet and makes off. She passes under some belahs to the shrill sound of the westerly in leafless branchlets, but the trees are too widely spaced to be any protection, as are the leopard woods farther on. She maintains her course successfully in spite of the pressure of the wind and the constant nudging of Merloo, who is so intent on keeping under her lee that his plum-colored body is often hidden and only his pale, almost white, hind legs, taking two hops to her one, are visible.

When they do reach the low ridge of red sand the cover

is poor. Most dark and distant barriers of vegetation on a plain finally resolve themselves upon closer acquaintance into nothing more than a sprinkling of solitary trees and bushes and seldom into woodland of any consequence. Nevertheless, there are trees, often gnarled and straggly, and some tufts of windmill grass.

Wangarie stops in the shade of a leopard wood whose foliage is trailing beards of mistletoe. Merloo nuzzles her, so she remains on her feet until he has pulled the mouth of her pouch open and put in his head. While he is drinking she combs him with her forepaws.

It is hot on the sand ridge, the wind out of the west having warmed the day considerably. The young buck who was under the same tree as Wangarie and Merloo hops slowly by without noticing them. It is doubtful that he is still at heel, because it has been six months since he was last suckled by his dam, the youngest of the blue flyers in the group, who at present is grazing far out on the plain. Her new joey has been taking a good look at the world lately and will soon be leaving the pouch for short periods. Today, finding the wind unpleasant, he is detectable only as a bulge. The doe is now almost wholly indifferent to her previous offspring, as he is to her except when the group is on the move or there is a threat of danger.

Other kangaroos are sheltering on the sand ridge, including a big gray buck somewhat darker than the eastern grays, or gray foresters. His head and neck are almost black. He is a western gray, and he has wandered to the most northwesterly point of the range of his species.

The wind has lost much of its persistence when the

kangaroos return to the plain to feed in the late afternoon. Some more reds and a thin scattering of gray foresters have appeared, but there is only one western gray. He is tall, gaunt, and slow, and the greater part of his life now is spent in feeding—more than in sleeping. He is so old that his incisors are no longer effective and he is forced to tear at the tussocky grass with sideways jerks of his head. Even then, having won a mouthful, he is unable to chew it properly because he has only two molars left, and these are so badly worn as to be virtually useless. Often staggering from weakness, the old western buck has not many days to live.

The other kangaroos move on. Having seen scarcely any sheep for two weeks they suddenly happen on a number of them. This isn't so coincidental, for red kangaroos have such a distinct preference for short green grass that they often search out country that has been cropped by sheep.

May, so far, has been a gentle month, and this particular late afternoon has become as placid as the windy days were boisterous. A golden veil of dust films the sky around the horizon, and there is a soft breeze. Practically indistinguishable from the innumerable low bushes humped against the sinking sun, the sheep and the kangaroos drift slowly on. Sometimes a kangaroo will stand up alertly—a tall triangle surmounted by great ears—then descend again into the multitude of forms; the quiet is not broken until some black cockatoos on their way to the river settle in a cluster of belahs. A clamorous company with wings fanning and the red feathers of their tails flashing, they balance awhile on the broomlike foliage before flying off again

68   [The Year of the Kangaroo]

without feeding. Rising and falling buoyantly, they go on toward the river where the tops of their roosting trees are sketched against the sky.

The eighteen-month-old buck in Wangarie's group, who sometimes stays close to his parent but generally does not, has found the company of two youngsters of his own age and sex, and soon a three-cornered sparring match has started. Meanwhile, the cosmic footlights under the western horizon are changing the golden dust-laden sky from color to color until a pale, translucent green is merging at last into the deep, electric blue of approaching night. Before it is dark, however, one of the players, finding the game too rough, turns away, thus bringing the show to an end.

That night Merloo hears the cry of the barking owl for the first time. It comes from a tree close by, and he crowds fearfully against his parent. The other unusual sound is very faint, only just within earshot—within the range of a kangaroo's hearing—a rifle shot tapping the quiet. It is followed by another and then, again, after an interval, another. But the shooter is so far away that there is no other sign of his existence, no glint, no faint reflection of a light or murmur of a motor.

The marksman lining his sights on the chest of the buck kangaroo sitting up and staring, transfixed, into the brain-piercing glare of a spotlight squeezes steadily on the trigger. The butt jerks against his cheek and the kangaroo slumps. It always amazes him—the speed with which an animal, killed instantly, collapses. Seems to hurl itself into the grass and vanish. Probably the simultaneous relaxation of every nerve, muscle, and sinew. Like turning off a fountain.

The explosion, that insult to the night, is something the target animal never heard. Yet, as the spotlight is switched off, its echoes still seem to be racketing away into the silence—like the crashing of steel plates on a concrete floor.

Dr. William Cable works the bolt back and forth, pockets a live shell, and puts the rifle down.

"That's the lot," he says, relieved.

"Never knew what 'it 'im," his companion assures him consolingly. "You're getting to be a good shot, Bill."

Bill Cable knows that, frankly, he is not a good shot. That is why he always gets so close to the quarry and always insists on resting his rifle on some part of the truck after the motor has been turned off. He is not a skilled kangaroo shooter in the professional sense and does not pretend to be. His tally is eight a week, every week, rain, hail, or shine. He never shoots more than eight, that being the number of specimens he requires for a special study of the food preferences of kangaroos throughout the four seasons.

Joe Valetti, his assistant, tactful friend, and admirer of six months' standing, lifts a metal container out of the vehicle. Bill Cable takes a knife and a ball of twine, and they start walking. There is no need for a flashlight until they are standing over the victim.

The kangaroo's eyes are open. A soft breeze is causing its fur to quiver. Cable fills his pipe and lights it. Better to get a pipe going before starting the post-mortem; then there is no need to be messing around wiping and washing your hands if you want a puff later. Joe waits, knowing that his companion always allows a few extra minutes to go by to make sure the animal is dead. You don't work alongside a man, even if he is a doctor of zoology or biology or something, without getting an idea of his thoughts. Idly, Joe directs the flashlight beam beyond the immediate scene and it catches the red glints of kangaroos' eyes watching from farther out.

"You'd think they'd be miles away by this," he mutters.

Once started on the job Bill is pretty slick, though, and Joe has to admire him. It is a privilege to know a joker like Bill. Clever cove, too, but nothing flash about him. "Call me Bill," he had said, first day up from Canberra.

"What the hell's wrong with you? Can't you keep the bloody light straight?"

"Sorry, Bill. How's 'at?"

Bill only lets out a cloud of smoke and thrusts his hand in again, seemingly rearranging the kangaroo's insides. Joe passes him a short length of twine and, after a certain amount of tying and cutting, the required portions of the gut and the gall bladder and tract are lifted out and dropped into the metal container.

The two men make their way back to their moon-glazed truck. Joe puts the container with the other three. He chalks "B7" on the side—buck about seven years old. Cable always ages the specimens by the condition of their teeth.

As they are driving toward the nearest track Joe turns off the headlights, and their range of vision widens. Ahead and on either side the low, rounded bushes covering the plain look like cobblestones in a giant's courtyard. Joe maintains it's easier to drive without headlights when the moon is bright.

"Stop awhile, Joe."

"Something wrong?"

"No. Just stop."

The vehicle comes to a standstill and Cable gets out.

"I was wondering what a man would see and hear if he were by himself."

"Won't hear much." Joe grins, switching off the motor. "Might hear a sheep—maybe. If there's any about. Or you might hear some ducks flyin' over, from one tank to another, or makin' back to the river. Might hear a fox bark. 'Spossible. But, most likely, you won't hear nothin'."

Cable walks away a few steps and stands still, and that *is* what he hears, sure enough, nothing. So quiet. Eerie. No, not eerie—serene. Tick, tick, the cooling motor interrupts, mundane as a clock. He walks on until the sound fades, and looks up again. Not only serene, but sublime, too. He turns slowly, full circle, overwhelmed by the quiet and the light pouring down; feeling, for one dazed moment, that he is falling into space.

Then they are bumping on their way again to the noise of the motor and the rattle of tins in the back.

It is eleven o'clock when they reach the base that has been set up in the northwest of New South Wales for the Australian Department of Industrial Research. The diesel engine supplying the current for electric light and refrigeration automatically turns on as they are carrying in the tins. Joe puts them into cold storage for examination later.

Eighteen months of sifting through the stomach contents of kangaroos and sheep has provided Cable with records and comparisons that, up to the present, indicate that the diet of the two kinds of animals, although very much alike in the main, show certain marked differences. He has discovered, contrary to his expectation, that sheep browse more than red kangaroos, who prefer grass and generally seem able to find it—short, green grass, at that—as well as fleshy plants like pigweed. Although red kangaroos browsed as freely as the grays during a dry spell, that was a matter of necessity.

Cable's work so far has also shown that kangaroos and sheep eat about the same amount—a finding that should explode the fable that one kangaroo eats as much as three sheep. Red kangaroos may take longer than sheep to eat a given quantity of food because they are pickers, but Cable is already sure that their appetites are the same.

Another part of the research being carried out from the same center is based on the marking of individual kangaroos in order to find out how far they wander or whether they tend to remain in the same place. Although this work is in its early stages, it seems that kangaroos become wanderers only when food in their neighborhood is scarce. Restless creatures by nature, their journeys are mostly around the same locality—except during a drought, and then they often cover considerable distances in search of pasture.

They have a penchant for arriving at the scene of a thunderstorm to eat most of the green shoots before the sheep can get there—supposing the new growth to be within the traveling range of sheep.

Cable deduces from this that red kangaroos can thrive in

arid regions where domestic stock would perish. Red kangaroos are naturally conditioned to such places because they have lived there for so long.

Where the climate is excessively hot, kangaroos feed at night and rest in the shade all day, thus conserving moisture and energy. Furthermore, after ages of living under arid conditions, kangaroos have evolved an ability to void a high concentration of bodily waste in a small volume of urine, an additional help in solving the problem of dehydration in hot and waterless regions. Their extreme mobility serves them, too. Quite often they will appear on the scene of a faraway storm before the young grass has wilted and died off, and in this way they graze at least some of that ephemeral pasture that, because of the heat and the absence of drinking points, is well beyond the reach of sheep and cattle.

It is the kangaroo's mobility combined with, and largely depending upon, its ability to exist without water that most enrages the grazier whenever a storm on his property produces a green shoot and a multitude of kangaroos from adjoining properties to eat it. Even those men who are prepared to carry a proportion of kangaroos on their land—and such tolerance among graziers is by no means rare—feel that an influx of native herbivores on such a scale is really more than they as private citizens should be asked to bear.

Although the behavior of kangaroos under drought conditions is part of Cable's work, it is, to some extent, secondary. There is much to be learned about the effects of drought on kangaroos, especially since their diet changes in dry times, and it is one of Cable's suspicions that kangaroos cannot live as long as sheep on poor dry feed, provided there is water for both. He is determined to investigate this also, as soon as he gets the opportunity.

In the meantime he is studying the movements of kangaroos in fair seasons. To do this he has built yards around the earth tanks in the selected region to trap temporarily, for the purpose of banding, any animals that come to drink.

The use of tranquilizing darts was considered as an alternative to trapping but was not tried because the odd shape of the kangaroo makes it a difficult target for a missile of somewhat erratic flight. A dart must be shot into a thick and meaty part if the subject is not to be injured. And there's the rub! For a kangaroo is an extremely lean and, considering its size, a rather fragile creature. It has no well-padded rump, and to try to shoot a dart into the tail of a bounding kangaroo would be next to impossible. This leaves the hind legs, or haunches, and even there it is adequately fleshed only near the butt of the tail. So Cable finally adopted the trapping method.

The building of the yards and the provision of a spring-loaded gate for each yard was not started until he was convinced that there was no better way. Before that he had even allowed himself to be persuaded by two young zoologists from the headquarters of the department in Canberra that it should be possible—in fact, fairly easy—to run down a red kangaroo if a good, zippy vehicle was available. After three days of swirling over the dusty plains during the summer before last, the young men had indeed proved that it *was* possible. But they also had proved that it was not only not easy but dangerous, exhausting, and time-consuming. After several hair-raising pursuits they had caught four kangaroos and another had dropped dead. Admittedly, one of the four captured was a blue flyer, but all the conditions had been against her. They had managed to surprise her in the middle of a very wide plain where the grass was short and the black soil surface free of eroded gutters and crab holes.

They timed her at seventy kilometers an hour, and when they wanted to turn her they generally had to do seventy-five. Cable reckoned that if they hit a hole at that pace they would turn over. He marveled at her speed and grace. He watched her head especially; it might have been running on rails along the horizon. He marveled at her agility, the way she dodged when they tried to cut her off, and he marveled at her endurance. Either her pouch was empty or contained a young one too small to affect the performance of its parent.

Cable was about to call the chase off, as much for his own sake as the doe's, when she swerved and, in trying to dodge the vehicle, which had also changed course, tumbled head over heels and slithered to a stop. They grabbed her and prepared for a struggle, but there was none. She was exhausted. While Cable's helpers fastened a plastic band loosely around her neck the scientist examined her pouch and found a joey of only a week to ten days old attached to one of her teats. When they released her she lay there gasping, her flanks heaving and her lower jaw hanging slack.

The men drove away, then watched from a distance. Cable used his field glasses. It was minutes before the blue flyer got to her feet and, sitting back on her haunches, started to lick her forearms to cool herself. She was salivating copiously and her fur was soon saturated.

"Three youngish bucks and a doe for three days' work. It's no proposition," was Cable's summing-up. "Wear and tear on the truck, wear and tear on my nerves, a dislocated vertebra, plus the risk of being pitched out at any moment to say nothing of overturning. Back to base!"

Then they came upon a big old buck lying under a coolabah tree. If he had not started up as they drove by they might not have noticed him—but the track passed so close that his nerve gave. So he moved out into the sunshine. It was noon and the metalwork of the truck was too hot to touch. Standing up to his full height, staring at them, he stayed so still he might have been a termite's mound in the red country. No one in the whole wide world could have guessed that his heart was sick.

"It might be a good method for catching old bucks, all the same," the driver said. He was a little disappointed that his idea had not worked out very well in the case of the blue flyer. "What about if we try to grab this cove? He'd be pretty slow."

"Okay," Cable grudgingly agreed.

As far as he was concerned the method was hopeless. But he had been young, too, and, after all, it was on the way back. So they set out after him. He was not fast and they were soon right on his tail. Then he dropped dead and that settled it.

That night—nearly two years ago now—Cable had put in an order for the steel posts and netting and they went straight ahead with the fencing-in of five earth tanks, a blue, a red, a white, a green, and a yellow. Today the whole program is nearly complete. A white neckband has been taken from a dead kangaroo caught up in a fence two hundred and fifty kilometers west, and a green band has been returned by a kangaroo shooter who had been operating near the Queensland border. Many other sightings have been made within a radius of fifty kilometers.

After his own years of practical scientific work and hundreds of hours spent in studying the views of other men, Cable has come to the conclusion that it is impossible to form an Australia-wide picture of the relationship between the kangaroo and the man on the land. The dispersions and concentrations of the kangaroo population as dictated by the seasons are in themselves extraordinarily complicated. Also, the fact that red kangaroos cease to breed when a certain level of dryness is reached is another factor to consider in addition to the deaths from starvation. Nor does the sighting of a huge mob mean that there are other such mobs around. There may not be another kangaroo for a radius of thirty kilometers. But it does mean that the professional shooter, whether he is shooting for the fur and carcass market or thinning out concentrations of animals that have reached pest proportions, will be able to mark up large tallies in certain localities while the drought conditions last. It is the ebb and flow of the kangaroo population according to the appearance and disappearance of its food in good and bad seasons that make it so difficult to arrive at a total figure. Of course, it is never known how long droughts will last—or, if a season is good, how long it will remain so. How many sheep to the hectare should a grazier carry, irrespective of kangaroos? Should he stock up to the limit of good seasons, average seasons, or bad seasons? What is the average season?

Cable does not pretend to know all the answers. He feels, however, that both the red kangaroos and the gray foresters—in fact, all the big kangaroos, including the wallaroos and euros—are more numerous today than ever before. It is the smaller kangaroos that have suffered most. Formerly, there were more wallabies and pademelons and fewer of the large species. Now, because of the removal of natural cover, that position has been reversed. Also, the removal of much of the drought-resistant vegetation to make more country available for grass has not only greatly reduced the habitat of the smaller species but has also denuded wide areas of those native bushes that, although low in nutrient, have for thousands of years served as a buffer between good seasons and bad. The provision of more pasture and watering points for sheep and cattle has also benefited the large, highly mobile kangaroos, who are able to outdistance most pursuers, either on the plains where the red kangaroos live or through the woodlands and remaining belts of scrub where the gray foresters take refuge.

There are, consequently, quick expansions of numbers when sufficient feed is available and disastrous losses when the rains fail—as they always do, sooner or later.

Cable knows that there are arguments against many of his views as well as arguments for them and that it is his duty, at present, to discover facts. Statements could come later. But he had to start thinking and reasoning somewhere, even if it meant he would have to recast most of his ideas before he was finished. Still, even if there were no kangaroos, the policy of clearing all the native shrubs from semi-arid country to make room for more high-nutrient grasses that cannot stand up to dry, hot weather is surely unwise. Not that every grazier would adopt such a line; but some have, to their undoing. After all, if a drought is severe enough, everything dies—although it is undeniable that stock will live longer if there are no kangaroos to compete for the last wisps of food.

Cable believes in the importance of his work, the more so because he sympathizes with the various viewpoints of those concerned. He sympathizes with those who hate to think of kangaroos, any kangaroos, being killed and he sympathizes with those who, having a living to make, maintain that any living thing, humans excepted, that interferes with their object should be liquidated. He especially sympathizes with the grazier and farmer who like to have kangaroos on their properties in reasonable numbers but who are subjected to periodic invasions. Cable is inclined to discount reports of the extent of the damage done to fences by kangaroos, although he believes that farmers suffer more than graziers from this kind of expense. Once a hole has been made in a fence all the kangaroos in that paddock use it. So, too, of course, do all the sheep; so one hole can nullify the value of a lot of fence.

Already his investigations have taught him it is quite unreasonable to expect a calm evaluation of the kangaroo problem from a farmer who has just discovered a mob of gray foresters in his wheat field. An uninvolved party

would probably sidestep by saying that perhaps the government should do something about it—and perhaps, in this
case, he would be right.

It is almost impossible to be completely impartial in
such a matter, even if one knows all the pros and cons.
And nobody knows all the pros or all the cons. Furthermore, many of those who know about some of the pros
will not admit the existence of any of the cons, and vice
versa. Only scientists can be impartial. Cable is impartial,
he tells himself, although in his heart of hearts he knows
he is not. He is not going to admit to anyone, not even to
himself, that he is pleased when he is able to prove some
native animal innocent of a specific charge and regretful
when he has to announce the verdict of guilty. But his job
is to run down all the facts he can flush and then display
them fairly. He is confident he can and will do this to the
best of his ability, whether the final result is to the satisfac-
tion of his other self or not.

Cable has reached the last stages of his present studies,
having only a month to go to finish his inspection of sheep
and kangaroo stomachs and the banding of kangaroos
trapped in the yards built around the earth tanks. He has
also forwarded a number of gall bladders to a fellow scientist working on tapeworms in kangaroos.

Being rather tired by now of collisions with panic-
stricken animals in the catching yards, he is in excellent
spirits as he sets out with his assistant and general handyman, Joe Valetti, to make what may be the last round of
the earth tanks. With luck, no unbanded animals will
have found their way in tonight, so the men will only have
to note down the colors and the marks on the bands. They

can do that from outside the fence. Alan Havisham, a young agronomist who has been carrying out some special work on grasses for the Department of Agriculture, goes with them. Cable and he often confer over fragments of vegetable matter found in the stomachs of sheep and kangaroos under examination. Alan is a hefty youngster and enjoys tussling with kangaroos.

It is a beautiful moonlit night very like the previous night when Cable and Joe shot their half-weekly tally of four kangaroos, and there are twelve captives in the yellow yard. Eight are wearing yellow bands, two are wearing blue, and two are unbanded. The old blue flyer is there as usual. She seems to drink every night and has become so used to being trapped that she scarcely takes any notice of the men. She is waiting by the gate. When Cable opens it she goes out. She has recently lost her joey, who would now be at heel if he were alive. Knowing the heavy mortality rate of young kangaroos, Cable realizes the young one may have met with any one of a dozen fates.

After noting the particular signs on the bands and the colors, the men prepare to go in. The presence of two blue bands is not especially interesting, for the "blue" tank is only a kilometer away. The frequency of the visits by different animals is more significant. Some drink only occasionally, even during a fairly dry spell; others may drink two or three times a week. The old blue flyer drinks nearly every night. When green feed is plentiful some never drink at all.

The men go in, and immediately the yard is full of muscular projectiles as the terrified kangaroos, dazed by the electric lights, charge blindly about, repeatedly crashing into the fence and being hurled back to go plunging away again in some other random direction the moment their feet touch the ground.

Noises come out of a rising fog of dust—twangings and rattlings of the netting fence, furious guttural sounds from the kangaroos, and their less frequent hissing cries, as well as the thumping of their pads and an occasional shout of protest when a kangaroo collides with a man instead of the fence or another kangaroo. Cable is hit in the back by a flying doe. He makes a grab at her but is knocked aside by a buck rebounding from the wire. Hell, he's getting too old for this sort of thing! But Alan has got her. Joe shines the light in her eyes, but Alan is holding her without much difficulty. Cable fastens a yellow band around her neck. When Alan lets her go she leaps straight at the light, and Joe ducks just in time.

Now for the red buck! Once again it is Alan—agile, strong, and young—who gets him. The buck bounces up and down but Alan is hanging on to his tail like an anchor man in a tug-o'-war. Cable dazzles the buck with his light, and Joe makes his approach from the front. He is holding the band stretched out, one end in each hand.

"From the back, the back. From the back," Cable directs sharply.

Obediently making a detour, Joe fastens the band from the back.

"You ought to know the rules by this time," Cable snaps at him.

"He can't kick while Alan's got 'im by the tail."

"No, but he can scratch your face off."

The lights go out and the men leave the yard, propping the gate back. The dust rolls away; the kangaroos bound into the open.

Cable watches until they are lost in the mist of moonlight. That none of them has ever jumped the two-meter-high fence around the catching yard is not remarkable considering the frantic state of the captives, but why do so many of them fail to clear the ordinary paddock fences used to enclose sheep? He could just about jump over them himself. He has never been able to accept the easy explanation that not every kangaroo is a good jumper. Might as well believe that not every fish is a good swimmer. Unquestionably some kangaroos must be better jumpers than others, but Cable once saw a sizable buck, surprised in broad daylight, clear a two-and-a-half-meter fence from a standing start, so surely no kangaroo—except the aged and the very young—would have any difficulty with a fence only waist-high to a man. He is of the opinion that kangaroos, even when not pressed by a pursuer, confuse the thinness of wire with the wispiness of grass and that only some of those lucky enough to survive many crashes ever learn to make sure of sailing over that otherwise disastrous top strand.

Like other wild animals, kangaroos never exert themselves unnecessarily. They do not leap spectacularly over the grass tops when they can swish through them, and they do not travel at their best speed when they can make their own pace. A blue flyer, said to be the fleetest of the kangaroos, may reach sixty-five kilometers an hour when pursued, a buck perhaps sixty. The flyer can maintain her pace for longer than the buck, but neither lasts if hard pressed. The buck would probably be showing signs of distress after two kilometers, the flyer, if unburdened by a joey, in three or four.

On the other hand kangaroos can keep going all day at a casual twenty kilometers an hour, and the length of their hops at that easy gait would be only one and one-half to two meters.

It is hard to estimate the height a kangaroo can jump since most of the high objects that a kangaroo cannot go around are fences, and kangaroos seldom try to jump fences unless they are pursued—when they are so frightened that they generally crash into them without any attempt to rise.

There are reports of leaps of over three meters in height and eight meters in length, but these are usually made over fallen trees, brushwood, or other natural obstacles and are difficult to assess accurately.

No reference to jumping would be complete without some mention of the wallaroo. Not being roamers, wallaroos always use the same paths to and from the top of the scree as evidenced by the polishing effect of their paws. Wallaroos always know the way, which is one reason why a startled buck scooting up a rocky hillside is a sight that has to be seen to be believed.

It is late when Cable's working party arrives back at its quarters after having visited the other four enclosed earth tanks. Fortunately, there were only three more "strangers" to be dealt with.

The younger of the two mature bucks in Wangarie's group is seen to have a yellow band around his neck when he is feeding on the plain near some of the other members in the morning. There are now only seven kangaroos in the small company, the nineteen-month-old male-at-heel having wandered off with two others of his own age to make a trio of independent young bucks.

June

OLD MAN RED and a younger buck are basking on a sand ridge—a sand ridge so nearly level with the general flatness that it is a ridge in name only. If it were not for its trees it would be invisible, for it is the trees that turn it into an islet in an ocean of long grass—quite clearly, the only one in sight. Animal tracks meander between belah and cypress pine, and there are hollows and paw scrapes where sand has been thrown into the air when the flies became too worrying.

The smaller kangaroo has a yellow collar, the constant glittering of its plasticized surface not seeming to disturb or even to interest him or his neighbor. The rest of the group has left the sand ridge. Wangarie and the oldest of the blue flyers are dozing out on the plain, their offspring racing around them; but such dodgings and chasings are too lively to last, and soon the four are lying companionably together. Both young-at-heel stay very close to their mothers. They are not yet fully weaned, and although they spend some hours of every twenty-four in grazing, they are also suckled at regular intervals. Merloo, at ten months old, and slightly the younger of the two, is fast outgrowing the female and is already noticeably taller. He stands over a meter high, and both he and the female joey seem to be all legs. He weighs nine kilograms, compared with Wangarie's twenty-eight.

The third, and youngest, of the mature does has also moved away from the sand ridge and is lying in the middle of a claypan, where the warmth of the bare ground on this sunshiny winter's day is making her position almost too hot for comfort. Her fur has lost the tinge of red it had last season and has become smoother as well as more definitely blue. In a month or so the joey balancing unsteadily beside her will be leaving her pouch for good, and to judge from her present weakness the little creature will have to gain strength quickly if she is to have a chance of reaching maturity. With her spindly hind legs and uncertain gait and her thin, bony shoulders and forelimbs she looks, and is, absolutely dependent on her parent for her existence.

For the next two months or so she will run more and more of a risk every time she leaves her mother's pouch— which she must do, however, if she is to develop. She is now between six and seven months old, and it will be as long again before she will be fast enough to have any chance of escaping a pursuer. A sudden fright could send the blue flyer, always prone to panic, speeding off in an instant and, even if the deserted joey was not taken by a predator, the possibility of mother and daughter finding each other again would be remote.

Sprawled on her back, the blue doe thoroughly warms her chest and belly, then, turning on her side and propping herself on an elbow, tosses up a puff of yellow dust she has scratched from the hard surface of the claypan. She keeps on doing this until she has dug a furrow, when the puffs become bigger. Her joey hops erratically toward her. She is reddish on the head and at the base of the tail, with a bluish red back. Her hind legs are so pale that she appears to be wearing white stockings. When she puts her head into her mother's pouch to drink, the blue flyer takes the opportunity to lick her back and head clean of the dust that has drifted over her and to groom her with her forepaws. Then the joey burrows into her pouch until only her hind feet and gray tail are visible, they too disappearing as she struggles to complete a slow somersault. Finally her head reappears, all eyes and ears.

A storm is gathering in the northwest. It may come to nothing, although the clouds in the distance have already darkened to so nearly the same color as the river red gums along the Darling that the white cockatoos watching from their high branches seem to be perching on air.

There are three cockatoos in the trees, and they can be seen from a long way off, especially when they stretch their great, snowy wings. Yesterday there were seven; today, in the early morning, there were only two for a while, until they were joined by another. Every so often a sort of casual, unplanned changing of the guard takes place, as happens when one of the watchers planes down to the ground and white wings flare out of the grass as four others fly up to settle on the sticks spearing out of the red gums' foliage.

For two days the sentinels have sighted nothing untoward, but in the late afternoon of that day they suddenly beat into the air, screaming; they continue to scream and to circle above the dazzling host rising out of the grass beneath them. The din is stupendous as every bird, with wide-open beak and yellow crest erected, adds its own alarm call to the torrent of noise. A blue flyer lifts her head and peers toward the river but loses interest as the cockatoos, slow wing strokes flashing back the sun, recede into the silence of the plains.

It is only then that the kangaroos hear the sound of the motor that put the birds to flight, and they immediately set off toward the river. When an old-model sedan comes into sight and, by abruptly swinging in a new direction, makes as though to intercept them, they veer away and quicken their pace. By quaint coincidence the track, rather like the road in *Alice through the Looking Glass*, gives another wriggle and continues the pursuit.

Ron Anderson is in search of a new center for his mobile chilling unit, since the number of kangaroos around his present location is down to the point where it has become difficult to operate profitably. He is not greatly interested in red kangaroos, although he is watching this group carefully. The little coves seem to have quite a lot of speed, too. He accelerates and the kangaroos do the same, the two young-at-heel bouncing along like scared rabbits. One of the blue flyers has a biggish joey in her pouch. She would probably drop him—or her—if she were pressed, so Anderson slows down. Just then the track swerves to avoid a sand patch, and the kangaroos go straight ahead, easing up as they dodge through the usual sprinkling of trees.

Anderson sticks to the track, which, he has been assured, will take him to where he wishes to go. He wants grays, not reds. The weight limits on reds makes them risky shooting. He had been intrigued to notice that a buck in the group had a yellow collar. It is the sixth he has seen, so the scientists from Canberra who asked him not to shoot any 'roos with collars must have been busy. You could hardly shoot any by mistake—unless you were a rotten shot. The collars flash like jewelry in the spotlight and are very conspicuous by day, too.

It would not have been safe to shoot any of that group because of weight, either, except the big buck. If they had been grays he would have wiped them out—not deliberately, but that is what would have happened, because the five full-grown ones were heavy enough to make the weight limit for grays and the young ones left would then have died since they were not yet old enough to fend for themselves.

There is a big belt of mulga along a bit farther, so he has heard, and it is supposed to be full of grays. He reaches the mulga shortly and decides to move his chilling unit along as soon as practicable. He is not sure how good the site will prove, but there are kangaroos around, and it could not be worse than the place he is leaving.

After emerging on the far side of the trees the red kangaroos come to a standstill to watch Anderson's car disappear. They do not move much farther on and stop altogether when they reach the edge of the mulga. There is plenty of grass and the weather is mild, so the kangaroos drink seldom—although the oldest of the blue flyers must have visited a tank at least once while in the area, because she is now wearing one of Cable's white identity collars.

Varying numbers of gray foresters come out of the mulga scrub to feed in the evenings and then melt away again soon after sunrise—unless rain is falling or the sky is clouded, when they may remain on the fringe of the open country.

In approaching its new territory the shooting outfit keeps well out on the plain until it is opposite the site where it will be set up. The line of vehicles swings around and, leaving the track, lurches over rough ground. The hired towtruck and the mobile chiller it is hauling are like a tug and a tramp steamer plowing through a heavy sea. A separate diesel motor for the supply of electricity for refrigeration is coupled to the chiller and blotted out by it. So are the owner's sedan and the truck bringing up the rear. The truck, fitted with lifting gear for easier evisceration of the slaughtered kangaroos, is in charge of Anderson's friend, offsider, and general handyman, Nat Mills.

The setting up of the plant does not involve much more than the unhooking of the towtruck, and within half an hour of its arrival the regular popping of the diesel motor's exhaust tells of the reduction of the temperature inside the chiller. The towtruck, having turned on its headlights, is completing its hundred-and-twenty-kilometer return trip to Cobar as Anderson and Nat Mills leave in the truck to test the possibilities of their new hunting ground. They are back in four hours with forty-three carcasses—twenty-three gray bucks, two red bucks, and eighteen gray does —which suggests to Anderson that he will have no difficulty in restoring his operations to a profitable basis.

The next night, as on the previous night, the shooters make sure of the biggest targets as soon as the spotlight is turned on. Naturally, these are bucks. By the time most of the bucks have been shot the mob is on the move and only four of the larger gray does are dead. Anderson shoots one red buck but, with the exception of three other bucks shot later in the operation, no other red kangaroo is included in the total for the simple reason that Anderson will not take the risk of killing any blue flyer not clearly an aged animal and well above the minimum weight. Any such blue flyer—and they are few and far between—will be shot by him, personally, or not at all, he says. It is the only way, he maintains, to keep underweight carcasses out of the picture and thus avoid any suspicion that he might be trying to circumvent the law.

The seven kangaroos in Wangarie's group move away from the crashing of rifles but not so far that they are out of earshot. Other red kangaroos join up with them to bring the total to twenty, including three young-at-heel; in the afternoon some foresters increase the size of the mob to seventy or so. Pausing to scan the plains before they finally quit the scrub, the foresters seem to vanish completely, so perfectly do they blend in with their background, which is grayish, too. A kangaroo at gaze is not a kangaroo but a weathered tree stump, or a reddish claypan in the distance, or a rounded blue bush. When the foresters at last decide to venture into the open it is as though some of the tree stumps move a fraction of a second before they are changed back into kangaroos.

They feed for an hour or so before they hear the drone of a motor and see the glow of headlights, when they start hopping away in various directions. But the night is overcast and they do not take fright. Their behavior is the same as on the previous two nights.

The spotlight picks out a broken line of grays, and a few reds, three or four deep along the edge of the mulga; and the pattern of the slaying is as usual, the kangaroos caught in the main glare sitting bolt upright, dazed, while those near the shadowy limits of the rays go blundering away into the dark. While the shooting is going on, some of the kangaroos stand up higher in alarm but do not otherwise move until they, too, drop with that macabre instantaneousness that never seems quite credible. None of them struggles, except one who manages to regain his feet and is immediately killed by a second shot.

Then, the panic. The light traverses and, finding no kangaroos, goes out. Momentarily the night is pitch black.

"We'll drive along thisaway," Anderson decides, with a jerk of his head. "There's a fence along here. It's broken down, but the corner's sound."

A burst from the spotlight after they have traveled a short distance shows the dim forms of kangaroos ahead, and the truck keeps to its course. Wangarie is caught up in a rush of fugitives, who break back toward the open plain—the oldest, biggest, and, therefore, the wariest of the bucks leading the way. When the spotlight is next switched on it reveals a mass of kangaroos, mostly grays, milling around in the netted corner.

"Mind that buck with the yellow collar," Anderson shouts between the crash of rifle shots. "And there's a flyer with a white collar," he says in low-voiced parentheses because of his oft-repeated instructions that blue flyers are not to be shot under any circumstances.

When there are no targets left they walk up to the fence. All the dead kangaroos are grays, bucks and does. There is a heap of them in the corner, and others are lying here and there against the netting. Gaps torn in the rusty wire show where some kangaroos charged through; a good many must have escaped when a surge of them broke back past the hunters. Of those who tried to jump the fence some were successful and some failed. A big, gray buck, held by the hind legs and pawing frantically at the ground

as he swings over the top wire, is dispatched by a single
blow from the cleaver used for removing the heads and
hind feet. Anderson cuts the throat of a doe in the same
way as a slaughterer kills a sheep. He also uses his knife to
end the lives of any joeys too small to have a chance of
surviving without their mothers. Every very young joey,
whether in the pouch or out of it, is destroyed—although
not every kangaroo shooter takes the trouble to do this.

Merloo is the last thing moving. Hopelessly enmeshed
he is by now struggling only feebly. Anderson grabs him
and holds him while the bloodied hands of Nat Mills free
his forepaws.

When Merloo is released he crashes into the netting
again but rebounds and, chancing to have been flung back
in such a manner as to be facing in the opposite direction,
vanishes into the darkness.

"He'll be all right if he can find his mum," Anderson
says.

After extricating the dead gray doe from the netting, the
men switch out the spotlight and start their butchering,
using the lifting gear on the truck for the evisceration of
the heavier animals. Then the carcasses are stacked on the
truck table top, or tray. Returning to the scene of their first
onslaught of the night they go through the same proce-
dure.

During this time Wangarie and Merloo are, of course,
separated; and the blue flyer is quite as agitated as her joey,
who has already tried to claim a gray doe and a gray buck
as his mother and been rebuffed by both. He is probably
not yet in much danger of being taken by any predator, the
disturbance of the shooting being too recent, but it will not
be long before foxes will be attracted to the scene. There

are many of them in the district, but the squeakings of the lost joey do not carry far.

Wangarie keeps bounding away in any direction that comes into her head, calling loudly. Sometimes she bounces abruptly to a halt and stands up high on her toes to call and call again, to listen and peer into the cloud-blanketed dark. Then she sets off as before, and by now her behavior has so affected the other two flyers that they are as agitated as she. They follow her, hard on her heels, wherever she goes, the elder of the two being followed in her turn by her own young-at-heel, now almost exhausted.

When Merloo hears their calls—or senses the vibrations of their thudding pads—he races toward them to be met and overwhelmed with nudgings and nuzzlings of their soft noses as they suck in the scent of his fur. Two of them soon turn away and the night's hysteria comes to an end with the safe reunion of mother and offspring.

Both mature bucks now leave the group, although Old Man Red, who is really imposing enough to be classed as a boomer, returns after a few days. The younger buck, now conspicuous because of his yellow identifying collar, is about to mate with a blue flyer attached to a mob drifting slowly west. In the larger mob there are other does almost ready to mate, and he will remain with them for the rest of the year, eventually swimming the Darling River to become an inhabitant of the drier regions on the fringes of the desert country.

The weather breaks toward the end of June, and the grasslands lose their definition as the gray rain shrouds them in grayness, too. Eroded earth gutters resound with the ripplings of running water, and often the beating of the rain is louder than the drone of the wind in the trees on the sand ridges. Because the black soil of the plains has turned into a gluey mass that clings to their feet and, being bound together by dead grass stems, builds up into great clods, the kangaroos shift to a mulga woodland where the ground is red and gravelly with patches of pure sand.

Much of the scrub in the district has been thinned by landholders in the same way as the area where the shooters started their operations. There are some sizable clearings, and these are favored by gray and red kangaroos alike because green shoots of new grass are often to be found there.

For a species with a definite breeding season in October and November, the joeys of the gray foresters vary widely in age. Most are still being carried, as would be expected since grays do not quit the maternal pouch as early as reds; but there are also some young-at-heel big enough to have been born four or five months before the last breeding season, no doubt because of the premature death of a joey from a previous mating.

After a while the red kangaroos cross a low ridge of cypress pine where the ground is drier, but thin indeed in pasture. As they emerge from the trees five wee jugglers, whose white wings seem to be lined with pink satin and who are perhaps the most beautiful of all cockatoos, fly up and float luminously against the overcast.

Beyond the cypress pines is a plain, its red, sandy distances hidden under an immense expanse of wallaby grass. There the red kangaroos graze under open skies until well after dark, when they return to the cypress pine belt to sleep.

Fine and frosty weather sets in after the rain. Winter, already a month late, has arrived.

July

HAVING BEEN almost wholly nocturnal throughout the warmer weather, the red kangaroos have become mainly diurnal with the onset of winter. In spite of the change, however, they show no sign of stirring on this particular morning, although the light is already tinged with sunshine and the coats of the sleepers have taken on their daytime colors.

There are again seven in the group, if the joey of nearly eight months is counted—she is just old enough to be permanently excluded from the parental pouch at any moment. She is huddled close to her mother.

The seven are somewhat crowded. It has been a fine, cold night and they are all lying under a wilga growing out on the plain. If it had been windy they would have sought the lee of a scrub-covered sand ridge, for the branches of the lone tree have been trimmed off as high as a sheep can reach. Most of the wilgas in that locality have been so trimmed and, although these provide good shade, the kangaroos prefer to camp under the occasional exception whose foliage, for some mysterious reason, is objectionable to stock. Such trees, trailing naturally on the ground, give coolness in summer and, in winter, warmth and shelter from the wind and driving rain; they offer concealment the year round.

Beyond the ceiling of leaves the ground is white with frost. It glitters between the grass tufts and crackles when Merloo ventures out. He does not go far and soon comes creeping back, a mess of icy soil and dead stalks sticking to his feet.

Right through the month so far the kangaroos have been studies in indolence, and their mood has not changed. There has been nothing to change it. Not yet hungry after their last grazing, they doze under their roof of wilga leaves and within their courtyard wall of high grass until a fly stings Old Man Red. His head jerks up, the sinews stand out on the arc of his neck, and he strikes angrily at his haunches. Instead of falling back to his former position, he props himself on his elbow and, using his free forepaw, puts up a fog of dust.

Getting to her feet Wangarie drags open her pouch with her forepaws and, bowing her back into three-quarters of a circle, licks her young one clean. It is now three months old and its fur is just starting to appear. Then she cleans the pouch itself and follows this by seizing Merloo, whom she grooms thoroughly and suckles. Both the remaining blue flyers, each with an empouched joey much larger than Wangarie's, are soon similarly occupied, the white plastic collar of one of them flashing like a heliograph as she licks the thickening coat on the small five-month-old leaning from her pouch.

The female joey belonging to the youngest of the flyers is curled up on the ground beside her mother when, for her, the grooming process starts. It has been a month since the slackening of her demands for milk gave the signal to the waiting blastocyst to resume its development forthwith; so it may well be that she has already had her last ride in a pouch. In fact, the birth of her successor occurs the next day, whereupon the flyer immediately stores up another dormant blastocyst by mating with the only mature buck in the vicinity at the time—Old Man Red.

As soon as they have been groomed and suckled, Merloo and the young doe-at-heel start gamboling wildly around the older kangaroos, bounding through the grass and rushing upon their parents and wrestling with them, then away again on a frantic, zig-zag course and back to the blue flyers. It is extraordinary how mildly the does accept these boisterous scufflings. Once in a while they may hit out protestingly, even angrily, but for the most part they simply close their eyes and, holding back their heads as far as they can out of harm's way, submit to buffet after buffet and collision after collision, not to mention frequent grabbings by the ears or tail by their exuberant offspring. The roughness of their play has steadily increased with their growth, and they are now almost a year old and already big enough to fend for themselves. However, they will probably stay with their parents for another six months or more after they have ceased to be suckled—a deprivation that cannot be very far away.

The grass that is growing strongly in most places varies considerably in height according to the nature of the soil. There are wide stretches where it is dense and short, and there are the yellow or red ocher claypans where there is little if any at all. But where Wangarie and the others of the group are resting, the tussocks are so tall that only the biggest bucks can look over them. In that paddock the red kangaroos of the plains are harder to see than the gray foresters in their woodlands and scrubs—a reversal of the usual situation since the grays, by reason of their habitat, are generally more difficult to spot than the reds.

Of course, the red kangaroo of the plains is not exactly conspicuous even when he is sitting up motionless on bare earth, because he always seems to blend as subtly into his own natural background as the gray blends into his. But, unlike the gray, he seldom has the additional advantage of partial concealment behind a tree or bush.

The owner of the property was reminded of this very matter when he tried to find out the number of kangaroos within his own boundaries in order to apply to the National Parks and Wildlife Service for a permit to thin them out. But counting in country that is divided up into paddocks is easy compared with counting in country where there are no restrictions on mobility.

In patchy seasons kangaroo populations are always shifting. During droughts and dry spells a single thundershower may attract all the kangaroos from counted areas for twenty kilometers around and concentrate them in some place where the count is about to start.

On the open plains red kangaroos can be counted from aircraft and pretty accurate results obtained as long as the pilot maintains sufficient altitude to avoid stampeding them into transects already flown. Even then, things can go wrong, and too often an exercise that begins as a head count quickly degenerates into an estimate and finishes up as a guess.

Because of the nature of their habitat any direct method of counting gray foresters is out of the question except in very sparse scrub, although general figures can be obtained by assessing the density of the kangaroos at so many to a unit of area. This figure may be based partly on counting, partly on the amount of food available, and partly on the scatter of droppings on feeding grounds.

On the sheep station where Wangarie is, however, an estimate of the number of kangaroos having been made, there are for the present no more scares or alarms—no shooting parties, no risk of a surprise attack by dingoes, now extinct in the region, no sudden outcry of feral dogs hunting in twos or threes, or any of those things that terrify a feeding or resting mob so that it literally flies to pieces. On such occasions the immediate response of the wild creature sends both bucks and does away before they know it. Their first few bounds are almost entirely uncontrolled, and any joey unlucky enough to be out of the pouch is abandoned. There is seldom any real attempt on the part of the mothers to recover their offspring. Quite often, too, the shock to the doe is so severe that a sizable youngster may be spilled out and the flyer gone in the same instant.

However, if a female kangaroo chances to catch sight of a predator at a distance she will carry her pouched young one with her when she flees. It is only when she is hard pressed and near exhaustion that her muscles relax sufficiently to allow the joey to fall out—although this would not happen if the joey was very small.

Although the attentiveness of a female kangaroo to her young in ordinary circumstances is unstinted, there are few instances of does defending their joeys in the face of danger. Nor do female kangaroos hide their young and return to recover them later when the coast is clear. If a doe is separated from her joey it will be only by good fortune that the two are ever reunited once they are out of earshot of one another. At the same time, the squeakings of a lost joey will bring every doe who can hear the cries at full tilt to the spot whether they have lost their own offspring or not and, similarly, a doe calling for her strayed youngling will always cause a good deal of agitation among other does in her company.

Day after day the weather stays fine, from cool to cold at night and then warming steadily until noon, when both the reds and the grays sunning themselves may hop sleepily to the nearest cover and collapse in the shade; the month remains tranquil until a stockman with a few kilometers of uneventful ambling behind him and a few more ahead of him urges his dogs to follow a scent they have just picked up.

So far neither the motorized buggy that passed by a few days ago nor the horseman at present jogging along the track has caused the kangaroos much concern. They are suspicious and watchful but they do not take off. It is the sudden appearance of the dogs that panics them.

As a diversion the man finds the incident disappointing. Dashing into the long grass, both dogs are not only immediately lost to view but also fail to notice two does racing through some open scrub to their right. The quarry the dogs are chasing is undoubtedly a big red, judging from the size of the back that surges above the grass tops every now and then, rather like a dolphin gamboling in a silvery sea. So there is no real chance of a kill—that is, of the kangaroo.

However, the stockman is treated to some moments of admiration as the blue flyers, coming suddenly upon a fallen tree, rise to a jump that would overtop a tall man and clear the obstacle with the grace and sureness of a pair of hunters. And he would have been more admiring still if he had known that one of the does was carrying a well-grown joey. He notices the white collar and, remembering that there is a scientific party working in the district, calls off the dogs with a whistle that also stops the blue flyers. They sit up and look back, electric with curiosity. Hidden in the long grass to the left of the track the dogs are already returning and now reappear with commendable promptness. They are not kangaroo dogs. They are sheep dogs and very obedient, which may explain why their pursuit of a big buck kangaroo was not only dutiful but circumspect.

When the month is nearly through, the weather changes. Clouds drift in from the northeast. Their advance is slow, their color white, and they are high up. Their rate of progress quickens as the wind becomes stronger and they darken and descend. At first the rain is as quiet as dingoes pattering over dead leaves, and the scent of wet dust rises. The sounds increase to a drumming on the ground, and the edge of the mulga scrub in the distance turns from black to gray. The wind grows colder and lashes the saturated kangaroos, so that the foresters retreat deeper into shelter and the kangaroos of the plains seek the sand ridges where clusters of casuarinas—mostly belah—provide some protection from the wind, if not the rain. The wind whistles through the needlelike branchlets of the belahs and the rain sprays through and streams down their trunks. Hollows in the red sand ridge overflow and the black soil plains turn to mud.

That night is pitch dark and the following day is evening from dawn to dusk. Galahs alighting on the sand ridge at noon are ashen hued. They pick up a few seeds before the wind whirls them away, screeching, their wings shedding water like smoke.

On the second night of the storm, Merloo, drenched ragged, is curled against Wangarie's side. The youngest of the blue flyers is under the lee of the same bush. She might have been colder if she had been out on the open plain catching the full force of the wind, but she could not possibly have been wetter. Her daughter-at-heel, now a week or so older than eight months, is sleeping with her nose buried in the familiar-smelling fur. Whenever she wakes she tries to suck, the joeys of all blue flyers being entitled by tradition to a further supply of milk after they have left the maternal pouch. It is really only the right of total, waterproof occupancy that has been withdrawn so far; however, her parent cannot be persuaded or forced to stand up.

The kangaroos can see nothing in the absolute dark, and most of the small sounds made by them are drowned out by the splashing of rain and the bluster of the wind in the belahs. So their respective identifying scents have a special significance for each other and especially for the young-at-heel. They communicate by the pressure of their bodies, too, and by the exchange of warmth.

The darkness is of the pit. But there the comparison ends, for a gale at night on the plains conveys no impression of chaos but rather of space. There is no turmoil of threshing branches as in a forest. Only the weight of the wind. When, at last, morning gleams through the clouds in the east it shows, dimly, the smallest of the joeys-at-heel with her head hidden in her parent's pouch. The blue flyer is standing up but crouching conveniently forward.

By noon the sun is shining out of a clear sky, and the wind, although continuing to blow coldly and steadily, has lost much of its force. The kangaroos start to feed and to move about again. Their main aversion is to the hot sun, and the sun will not be hot again until summertime.

August

OLD MAN RED, asleep on a sand ridge, lifts his head to stare into the dark. His throaty growl brings a blue flyer swiftly to her feet. She waits, poised for flight, while her small doe-at-heel, pressing hard against her and uttering a string of terrified, mouselike squeaks, informs the world at large of their exact whereabouts.

Leaves rustle as the fox goes, not as carefully as he came, and the musky smell of him fades. Always the hopeful opportunist, he would have hung around longer if the buck had not caught his scent. As it is, there is now nothing but to try his luck elsewhere.

The joey stops her whimpering. No bird calls, and the breeze is too slight to stir the brooms of the casuarinas standing black against the stars.

The kangaroos are still lying close when the dawn wind starts to blow, and they stay there until the sun is high. Then the wind changes, and they make for the leeward side of the shrubs and casuarinas.

Old Man Red stands up to take an observation. His ears are pricked, and although he seems to be intent on a particular spot in the distance, these signs of vigilance may be no more than the behavioral details of the alert posture he assumes from time to time when feeding. An itch in his lower ribs is sufficient to distract him and he bends his back, neck, and head in a luxurious sideways curve while he scratches the place with his forepaw.

When he and others of the group are grazing, their rounded backs are like six different-size turtles afloat in a sea of grass—three blue flyers, Merloo and the young doe who is his companion-at-heel, and the red buck. The seventh member is too small to be seen unless the observer happens to be very close.

Cloud shadows drift eastward throughout the morning, but the clouds are high and white. They have dispersed by afternoon, and the scene is again one of simplicity and peace—a blue sky, the plains, and a few animals grazing. The silence includes the murmur of the wind in the grass, and the wind has a keen edge to it.

It is some weeks since the red kangaroos saw another of their kind, and, since the mulga scrublands are beyond the southern horizon, there is little chance that they will come across any gray foresters while they remain so far out on the plains. Indeed, they have not glimpsed so much as a sheep. Feed is plentiful everywhere in the district, and sheep as well as kangaroos are widely dispersed.

Although the red buck must be aware of the others to some degree, he never seems to notice them and often grazes along a different line until he is out of sight. Sometimes he sleeps on the open plain when the does and young are sheltering on a sand ridge, and vice versa.

At present, the blue flyers with their young-at-heel are completely gregarious. They have found a spot where the wind cannot reach them because the grass is higher there, and they have been sunning themselves for the last two hours.

There is no movement until Wangarie hauls herself lethargically to her feet and swings her hind legs forward on the tripod of her forelimbs and tail. But she is not going anywhere. She combs the fur inside an ear, delicately, with the small, syndactylous claws of her hind foot, then swings herself forward again and droops there drowsily, her forepaws hanging just clear of the beaten-down grass. Her four-month-old is a bulge in her pouch. He has not seen the world yet, since he has never looked out of the pouch and his eyes were sealed when he made his short journey into it. He will make his first observation a month from now and will venture out for a short while in another month's time. Already his nakedness is covered with a skimpy fuzz of fur, which will rapidly increase in density and length. His crumpled ears will unfurl, and his tail and hind legs will lose what remains of their stubbiness. Wangarie closes her eyes, sighs heavily, and stretches out in the sun.

Soon after dusk a light appears and disappears in dots and dashes on the skyline. But it is so far away that there is no sound of a motor, and the year-old Merloo and the daughter of the doe with the white collar do not pause in their helter-skelter racing around the rest of the group.

The amount of noise their pads make in striking the ground is considerable because they are always dodging, and they often flatten a swath of the slippery grass as they slide in turning.

Merloo is finding it increasingly difficult to obtain suck, and the doe-at-heel, who is somewhat older than he, although smaller, is already resigned to the fact that she will have to keep herself alive in the future on herbage only, her mother's firming resistance having at last defeated her.

Merloo still wrestles with Wangarie, sometimes winning, sometimes losing. Lately he has been losing. Yet Wangarie and the blue flyer with the white collar are never vicious in checking their offspring and never use any but the most passive means of preventing them, either turning away, fending them off with their forepaws, or lying down. Both young-at-heel are now fully capable of grazing, having two premolars and one molar on each side of their top and bottom jaws, to give them twelve grinding teeth apiece.

Except for the events of a single morning, August is a tranquil month for the kangaroos. It is a somnolent month after a mild winter, and the rain has been fairly general even if it did not reach much farther west than another hundred kilometers. It is not lack of rain but a succession of frosty nights that has caused the brownness of the grass.

The good season and the consequent scattering far and wide of animals, both domesticated and wild, give the great sweeps of country their look of emptiness—empty not only of sheep and kangaroos, of feral pigs and goats, but also of birds.

Corellas and galahs are less often seen in the air and, of

course, are hidden by the grass when on the ground. Fewer waterfowl fly between the river and the earth tanks because the rain has transformed the depressions where clumps of reedy growth have survived the dry spell into shallow ponds full of aquatic insects and plants. When food is plentiful there is no more reason for birds to travel than there is for kangaroos and sheep.

Some days the group of red kangaroos sees no other sign of life than the sun glittering on a flock of corellas so far away that they look like scraps of silver paper fluttering down from the skies. Or, perhaps, only the big red buck sees them, for he does sit up now and then to stare around. He is warier than the blue flyers and not as curious. It is probably because he lacks their speed and endurance that he makes off immediately when he detects anything that might turn into danger. He seldom waits to make sure.

In four days nothing comes near them except five feral goats—two white kids and two white she-goats led by a black satanic male. They pass at a fast walk with scarcely a side glance at the kangaroos.

Clouds in the west start the red kangaroos drifting in that direction. There have been rain showers, and the kangaroos travel slowly, grazing as they go. They visit an earth tank on the way, since the brown grass of winter is deficient in moisture and they have not drunk for days.

To reach the paddock where the rain has fallen they have to put a fence or two behind them by floundering over the lower netted part and under the top wires. None of them attempts to jump. The grass in the paddock has been heavily cropped by sheep and is being spelled by the grazier. But the rain has brought up a green shoot and, to a red kangaroo, this kind of food is better than any other. Even the big red buck overcomes his fear of the insignificant-looking filaments which should offer no more resistance to his great weight and strength than the grass itself, even when it is as tall as he.

The red kangaroos are quite close to a homestead with its surrounding outbuildings and smaller paddocks—horse paddock, holding paddocks, and the like. One of the paddocks has been experimentally sown, and the crop that sprouted a week ago has been brought along quite remarkably by the rain. Gray foresters are feeding in the crop, which adjoins the paddock where the red kangaroos are nosing through the short grass for new shoots. In the morning when the red kangaroos head for the open plain, the foresters swing in the opposite direction, toward the mulga scrub, and go bobbing away through the faint ground mist like so many tappets, each idling rhythmically enough in its own way, although ludicrously out of kilter as a unit.

The following night when all the kangaroos return, the homestead is lighted and sounds of human voices and music thread through the outer silence. Always inclined to overestimate the protective power of darkness, the kangaroos merely pause awhile and then approach, the reds into the spelled paddock and the grays into the crop.

The number of red kangaroos feeding in the spelled paddock rises to twenty with the addition of a second, larger, group and a solitary buck. Only the blue flyer with the white collar fails to get through the fence. She does

not share the confidence of the others and soon moves farther away. Except for a final last loud twang of wire, Old
Man Red negotiates the fence as easily as on the previous
night.

Rain, fine enough to drift about like mist in the breeze,
is curtaining the paddocks. It dims the lights from the
house and softens the beat of the dance band. It closes
around the kangaroos crouched over their grazing and enhances the sweetness of the new grass. Neither the frag-
mented beams of turning headlights nor the honkings of
horns as the guests depart disturb the intruders. The eyes
of a blue flyer glow like coals as she sits up to stare back at
the brightness, but she is too far away to be seen from the
house. The last whiff of gasoline exhaust fades and there is
quiet, the coolness of wet earth, and the scent of warm,
damp fur. The soil of the plowed field sticks to the feet
of the gray foresters when they move. Some of them, fully
fed, crawl back through the fence; others lie down, and the
mud weights the bedraggled ends of their belly fur.

Dawn is not far away, although the night is as pitch
black as ever when a dog starts barking. A red kangaroo
gets up and goes, but Old Man Red does not stir. He has
eaten well, he is comfortable, and, in any case, a barking
dog is not something to strike terror into the heart of a
buck standing a head taller than a tall man.

A car engine roars, backfires, and stops. More dogs are
barking. Most of the kangaroos, red and gray, bounce to
their feet. Then two motors are running. Lights blaze, a
sharp voice calls the dogs back. It seems the chase is not
quite ready to start. It is not a well-organized chase. The

station owner had already written off his crop experiment as a failure, and this is to be more of a scare-off operation than a hunt.

Many of the kangaroos are slow to get underway, and Old Man Red is the first to reach the fence. Apparently he does not see it, perhaps because a spotlight suddenly alters the scene before him. He is traveling fast when he lands almost against the netting, and he no sooner leaves the ground on his next leap than his hind feet are checked by the top wires. The rest of him goes on. He cartwheels and slams down on his back. It is a majestic crash. But he is up in a moment, having suffered no damage other than the loss of some skin and a temporary disruption of his sense of direction. He pauses to stare into the glare of a spotlight now unaccountably in front of him, then comes around in an arc to the thunder of gunfire and heads for the open plains.

Some of the gray foresters have been caught on the fence of the plowed field by a party of shooters, and ten of them are hanging on the wires or huddled on the ground. Their killing has not been carried out as cleanly as would have been the case if professionals had been operating, but at last all movement ceases. The truck carrying the guns churns back to the house, while the other vehicle—a jalopy with a load of youths—trails after the red kangaroos and the dogs.

Despite his heavy fall and the distance lost during his moments of disorientation Old Man Red is well ahead of the rest of the fugitives with the exception of the white-collared doe, who would not follow her yearling offspring through the fence. But she had a long head start.

No red kangaroo was killed at the fence, and they are now scattering over the plain like light from a prism. The dogs are chasing Wangarie. They haven't the faintest chance of catching her, even though she is carrying a four-month-old joey. The way she sailed over the fence and the burst of speed she revealed when they rushed her should have shown them she was half again as fast as they; but they are an unschooled lot—and, at the moment, they have nothing else to chase. The surviving foresters are already in the deep scrub, and the other reds have disappeared into the misty dawn to the right and left.

At least the dogs can see Wangarie now that the light is strengthening. They start barking again. She turns her head and, frightened by that glimpse of dread, dingolike forms, increases her speed until the thud, thud, thud of her pads becomes a drumming sound and she seems to be running rather than bounding. Unless there are obstacles in their path, kangaroos do not jump high when traveling fast. Each low trajectory leap carries Wangarie about four and a half meters. Her speed reaches sixty-five kilometers an hour for a short distance but drops back to half that once she had drawn away from the dogs.

If the red buck had not moved the dogs would never have seen him. But he did move, somewhat reluctantly, for he is not yet rested. The dogs switch their attention to him and are after him just as energetically when full daylight comes. But they have not covered much ground. It has been a kangaroo-baiting match more than a chase.

The barking of the pack has never ceased, and if the men in the jalopy had arrived the quarry could have been finished off with a bullet. But the jalopy is in a bog and, as someone said, if they continue the chase it will soon be in another. So, no one being very keen to go on, everyone goes back. The dogs and the red buck stay pretty well where they are.

The big kangaroo is bleeding about the lower back and the butt of the tail. Although not seriously injured, he is starting to show the effects of the harassment of the pack. His eyes are glaring with anger, fear, and desperation—and anger is giving way to fear. It is difficult to feel any admiration for the tactics of the pack, but they are certainly effective against a cornered animal. The nerves of the red buck are breaking when the whole confusion of dogs and kangaroo splashes into a sheet of shallow water studded with clumps of reedy grass.

The dogs pause, disconcerted. They had been too intent on worrying their quarry to notice the pool the kangaroo was trying to reach, and there is a sudden quiet.

Past middle age, of great size, overweight, fully fed, and already tired out from bounding over the wet and gluey soil when the dogs had come upon him, the red buck is in bad straits. The present respite, brief though it may be, gives him a chance to recover his poise, if not his strength. He stands up straighter—two and a quarter meters—his curved talons again most obvious as they make threatening grabs at his enemies. Saliva drips from his jaws but the cast of his head is erect, his ears are laid back, and the fire has returned to his eyes. Drenched dark by rain, the rich redness of his coat is not apparent in the wan light of morning. He is black against the cloudy sky and looks all the more formidable for that.

The dogs circle him. They keep him turning. But it is

not the same. A dog attacks and is nearly caught as Old Man Red jumps forward and makes a grab. Uproar, and the shallow water churns to foam. Then a slowing of the action, a diminution in the amount of noise, a falling away in the ferocity of the hunters. One of them retreats to dry ground and stands there panting—rocking on his feet—tongue lolling.

The red buck licks his forearms and wrists. They are already wet with sweat and rain and the splashings they have received, but he licks them nevertheless—perhaps in an instinctive attempt to quiet his nerves. He shows no sign of trying to leave the water.

When the next attack comes it is half-hearted. Clearly, no support for the pack can be expected from the men who organized the hunt, and there is more space around the kangaroo when the spray next starts to fly.

Then Old Man Red has the biggest dog in his grasp. His teeth snap savagely at, but cannot reach, the kangaroo's throat, and the pack closes in as, deliberately, the red buck forces his prisoner under water. Neither all the clamor nor all the worrying will turn the buck from his purpose until the dog's muscled shoulders have ceased to twitch. He straightens up then, ripped and bloodied about his back and flanks and, suddenly, terrible—the glaring eyes, the laid-back ears, the slavering mouth, the grasping eagle's talons. But he will not leave the pool.

Not surprisingly his assailants retreat and pace up and down the muddied ground until the dog with the comparatively dry coat trots off in the direction of the homestead. One by one the others follow.

The kangaroo does not move for minutes. When he

does the swirl of his going causes the brindled markings of his victim to show momentarily, then the surface of the pool smooths.

Although none of the kangaroos in Wangarie's group has been killed, their number has decreased by two. The blue flyer with the white collar covered so much ground so fast that she lost touch with the others and never rejoined them. Promptly absorbed into a mob of thirty or so animals, she scarcely notices the absence of the daughter who failed to find her after the panic. Now a year old, the youngster will almost certainly survive.

However, the small joey who had just permanently left the pouch of the youngest of the three blue flyers is in a very different situation, since, besides being outdistanced by the grown kangaroos, she is not yet fully weaned. Separation from her parent, at the age of only thirty-six weeks, is for her a vastly more serious matter than it is for the yearling doe, and there is really no chance of her surviving.

Extreme fatigue keeps the red buck lounging around a low, sandy ridge on the plain for some days. He feeds and dozes and is soon contented enough to forget his own existence.

Except for the wind the weather is perfect. Nothing disturbing happens as, gradually and casually, the group reforms. If there were another scattering of its members it might never re-form, it is so small. Excluding young in the pouch there are now only five members left: two blue flyers, Wangarie and the young blue flyer who has just lost her very small joey-at-heel; two yearlings still at heel, the daughter of the flyer with the white collar and, of course,

Merloo, Wangarie's son; and, last and largest, Old Man Red. The company, then, is at its weakest numerically, especially since the big red buck occasionally shows signs of becoming a solitary. So August merges into September.

September

When the warmth of spring is added to the moisture left by the autumn and winter rain, the grass of the open plains soon grows tall enough to overtop the younger kangaroos and the blue flyers. Only the mature bucks are able to see the horizon, and most of them are obliged to stretch up to their full height on hind toes and tails' ends.

The size of Old Man Red is so exceptional that he is able to look over the grass tops while keeping the whole length of his hind feet flat on the ground, although for intense observation he always assumes the fighting three-point attitude.

It is early in a morning near the start of September, and the kangaroos are drenched with dew. As they move along, heads down and taking their smallest hops—a meter and a half in length and only half a meter high—which always seem so oddly mincing—the seed pods of the overhanging grasses douse them with water; the fact that they keep to the animal tracks does little to lessen the intensity of the showers. The trouble is that the pressure of the season's growth has so narrowed every pathway that the travelers cannot avoid brushing against the sides.

Three of the kangaroos—Wangarie, Merloo, and the yearling doe—arrive at some leopard woods as the sun rises. They are joined by the young blue flyer with the two-month-old suckling.

Old Man Red is sprawled out nearby. He is in his favorite position, propped on an elbow where the sun will dry him when it is higher. His long legs are crossed, his head is nodding sleepily, and a grass stalk is sticking out of his mouth. His attitude is absurdly manlike; his expression, if an animal can be said to have an expression, is surly. He seems manlike because he is lounging on his elbow, because his legs are plainly visible but his tail is not, and because of the grass stalk; he looks surly because of his half-closed eyes and because he *is* surly. He is not as young as he used to be. He takes no notice of the others as they pick their way through the leopard woods, and they take no notice of him.

There is quite a grove of leopard woods, a few of them in that early stage of development when they are mere tangles of branches strong enough to protect the central stem from browsing animals. It is hard to realize that the handsome, spotted trunk of every full-grown leopard wood sprang from such a mess.

The two blue flyers and the two yearlings groom themselves before they settle down, combing and nipping away seeds, burrs, and grass stalks from their wet fur. Wangarie cleans her pouch and licks the head and ears of her five-month-old joey as they are suddenly thrust out into the open air. The youngster has not yet left the pouch for even a moment and probably will not do so for another month.

The kangaroos make no sound other than the scratching of their ribs with their forepaws. All of them indulge frequently in this practice, which seems to be carried out more for the enjoyment of the scratcher rather than as part of the grooming process. Old Man Red, particularly, will often sit back with his spine recurved and his eyes closed and rasp away for minutes at a time. He is always the noisiest of the group because of the vigor of his scratching and the toughness of his hide.

Nothing really disturbs the peace of the kangaroos that day. Their dew-soaked fur soon dries, and the crying of ravens is so far away that it is distinct only when the breeze freshens; then, if the capful of wind should gather further strength, the brassy chorus is quickly blurred out by the rustling grass. Later, when a wedge-tailed eagle drops out of the sky, the protests of the ravens become clamorous and the kangaroos drowsily turn their ears elsewhere.

In the afternoon, closer to sunset than to midday, a low, guttural sound from the depths of the grass and a cascade of shrill chirps is followed by the appearance of an emu. Balanced motionless in the act of taking another step, the great bird, head raised high, fixes the kangaroos with one piercing eye and then, flicking his head through a hundred-and-eighty-degree pivot, with the other.

The light through the tree enhances the bright blue of his neck and the denseness of his filmy brown plumage— and he takes another step. Having taken another step he walks on as though the kangaroos no longer existed. He lowers his neck until his head is sailing in slow semicircles back and forth just above the ground, and at each downward jab of his beak a seed or a caterpillar or an insect vanishes.

Another guttural call brings nine or ten chicks into the open; they, being longitudinally striped and bright with sunlight, are like water eddying about their guardian's columnar legs.

When the emus leave the plain for the fringe of an expanse of mulga scrub, the brown form of the full-grown bird is ill-seen in the shadows. But their lighter colors and quick movements make the chicks conspicuous whenever they flash across a patch of sun, and their shrill voices are like points of brilliance in the gloom.

To the thudding of pads and the swish of branchlets swept aside, a party of western grays goes by, screened by the bushes. They are not traveling fast.

Western grays are not greatly different from gray foresters and here, in the west of New South Wales, the habitats of the two overlap. The western grays are rather darker than their eastern neighbors, and the contrast between their darker ventral surface and rather lighter frontal fur is not as definite. They are said to be more pugnacious than either the gray forester or the red kangaroo.

When they can see the plains through the scrub the western grays stop. Several young-at-heel are sprinkled through the mob, and some of them already have their heads in their parents' pouches. One young buck is nearly as big as the doe suckling him.

Most western gray females, like the gray foresters, suckle their offspring to the age of eighteen months and sometimes longer. If the young one being suckled is also a female the difference in size between parent and offspring is marked, but when the young-at-heel is a male he may well be taller than his mother. By comparison the female of the red kangaroo is usually done with suckling when her young-at-heel is a year old.

While the sun sinks the western grays wait. They have now advanced beyond the mulga trees and are sitting among outlying bushes and dead stumps. It is an ideal setting. Although no kangaroo is hidden, every one of them is practically unrecognizable.

Some are sitting next to or partly behind a stump, others are looking over bushes or peering through side branches, and all are motionless. To any eye but the most observant and knowledgeable they are invisible until the dusk starts to flow in like a tide. Then, out of nowhere a kangaroo hops forward, then another, then four or five more, and then the rest of them.

No rain falls in September, but a wind from the west in the middle of the month brings about a change in the environment. The wind is as low in moisture content as the deserts it has passed over—and they have been rainless for three years. So the grasslands begin to lose their last tinge of green. Small pools in gilgais and crab holes disappear and the muddy patches they leave behind crack into red or black tiles with curling edges. The trampled verges of the earth tanks dry as hard as concrete.

Although the wind usually dies away at night there is never any dew in the mornings. The sheep maintain their condition on the abundance of dry feed, and the kangaroos also continue to live easily in spite of the fact that green shoots are progressively harder to find. Some paddocks have already been turned into fire hazards, and the sight of a drover moving his flocks to a safer place is not unusual.

About a week before the end of the month the clarity of the northwestern sky is dimmed by smoke; but the grass fire is beyond the Darling River, and the wind is not so strong that a spark could be blown across. So the flames burn themselves out on the western bank, and the men keeping watch on the eastern side disperse.

It is only a few days since that part of the river was the scene of a stranger occurrence, when about seventy kangaroos had collected on the bank, among them the buck with the yellow band around his neck. He had then traveled seventy or so kilometers from the trap where he had been caught.

Sunshine slanting through the river red gums was mottling the steep east bank as the red kangaroos went creeping and sliding down the slope. Some paused at the edge to nose at the gray water; others plunged right in and started swimming. Not all of them began well, and there was some floundering when they found themselves out of their depth. Soon, though, they were going forward at a good rate by using their legs rather in the manner of a pacer. They seemed to be driven by some kind of mass urge. There was no obvious reason why such a crossing should have been made.

As the kangaroos emerged from the canyon of the river's banks the wet coats of the blue flyers, the plum-colored youngsters, and the red bucks gleamed in the rays of the sun.

After a while the number that had gained the western bank broke into smaller parties, which kept on dividing and coalescing, apparently at random, the only constant association being the obvious one of mother and offspring. As for the bucks, they went where fancy took them. No very old buck crossed the river. Male red kangaroos eventually become solitaries, if they last long enough—aged untouchables, haters of their kind, male and female, old and young, especially the young. Red bucks are old at sixteen years, and few attain the maximum age of twenty to twenty-three years.

When the grass on the west side of the river was set alight, by design or by accident, some of the red kangaroos were trapped in an arc of fire. Forced into the water again, they had no alternative but to swim back the way they had come.

Many of them, however, including the yellow-collared buck, stayed on the western side. The fire put the fear of death into him, too, but he had no difficulty in ultimately rounding the southern flank of the blaze, though he had to stretch his great legs to do it. No kangaroos moved farther than he, but the blue flyers moved faster. They were in a small party, and he and they passed and repassed repeatedly. Each time he passed them they were sitting up with their heads screwed around watching the smoke rolling up behind them or bouncing along very slowly, full of curiosity.

The yellow-collared buck kept going, the thud of his feet and the swish of the grass combining in a regular rhythm except when he was crossing a claypan. His gait was definitely undulatory, for he was well below his best speed; and, similarly, the blue flyers were bouncing higher than they would if they had been really exerting themselves. They, too, seemed to realize their course would be long. They often looked back from the top of a leap.

After consuming the grass between its starting point and the river, the fire burned slowly south as far as the boundary of the next property. By now the kangaroos have outflanked the flames and the buck is hopping leisurely alongside a fence marking the beginning of a semi-arid expanse, which has already been devastated by overstocking and wind erosion. He makes no attempt to get over or through the fence. Of the others also forced to the fringes of the same wilderness of red sand a few negotiate the fence each day until only four are left, the buck and three blue flyers. At last hunger drives them, too, under the wires.

There is scarcely any more feed on that side of the fence than there was in the burned-out area, but there is a watering point and they stay close to it. Fortunately the sun is not hot, because they seldom find any shade.

The clearing of the land in this instance has been a failure compounded by subsequent overstocking. Skeletons of bushes and mulga trees cast skimpy shadows across the red, wind-rippled sand, and the four kangaroos are able to keep themselves alive only by dint of continual foraging. There are never any green shoots, and all at once in the afternoon of a golden spring day the blue flyers set off toward the distant river. Bobbing away down the line of the fence they shrink gradually to a vanishing point.

Such a region as the one they are leaving could never support many grazing animals in its natural state, although the amount of grass growing there might well have been increased by a judicious thinning of the scrub. As it happens, the wholesale clearing that was carried out—which did in fact result in a considerable, but temporary, increase of grass—was really the start of the disaster, for it was followed by overstocking, a run of dry seasons, and devastation.

Everything died—the grass, the trees, bushes, stock, and kangaroos. But not all the kangaroos. The young-at-heel died, but some of their elders, by reason of their ability to travel long distances without drinking, reached places where there was both food and water.

Now, after the droughty years and a recent rain shower or two, the country is starting to recover. Patches of grass, a few bright desert flowers, and a ragged army of dwarf bushes have been seen. So, also, have some red kangaroos.

It is said that these kangaroos must be removed at once so that the process of regeneration will not be hindered. As there is no stock in the area, the poisoning of the waterholes is mooted by some landholders as being the cheapest and easiest method of extermination.

It was the poisoning proposal that brought the affair to the notice of the public. Various opinions have been, and are being, voiced, and the overriding comment is that the poisoning of waterholes is indefensible because the safety of creatures other than those at which the strategy is aimed cannot be assured.

Many other facets of the case are discussed—such as the heavy and continuing loss to the graziers whose properties have been so seriously damaged and the admitted fact that the devastation has been largely caused by an unsound plan for pasture improvement. Notwithstanding every pro and every con, however, the graziers' concern at the reappearance of red kangaroos is both real and intense. Their apprehensions cannot be allayed by scientific assurances that kangaroos do not deal as severely as sheep with poor-quality grazing land or that the combination of wholesale clearing, overstocking, and drought will again bring tragic results even if the nearest kangaroo is a thousand kilometers away.

As a preliminary to further argument and perhaps to gain a breathing space, the government asked the National Parks and Wildlife Service to count the kangaroos on the properties affected. The N.P. & W.S. then instructed one of its wildlife officers, Sam Johnson, to carry out the work. Having inspected the terrain, Sam decided on an aerial count as the only quick and satisfactory method, and by the time the fire started on the west side of the Darling the job was nearly done.

Because the properties were too extensive to be combed from boundary to boundary at acceptable cost to the service, separate grids of a quarter of the area were mapped out. Multiplying the count by four should then give an accurate total. Seemingly it would be a low figure, for when the aircraft landed to refuel after its first run, Sam forecast that the ultimate tally could be multiplied by any number up to twenty without finding enough kangaroos to warrant taking exterminatory action.

Two days later the tally of red kangaroos has risen to only fourteen, and the survey is nearly finished. It is late in the afternoon and Sam Johnson, wearied by hours of watching the ground within the boundary traced by an indicator on the starboard mainplane, is fascinated by the shadows of the wind-rippled sandhills and hollows.

Held to an altitude of one hundred meters, the plane

starts to turn for its last run. It is just as well that pilots never get sleepy, Johnson thinks—and spots a different shadow, a lanky shadow, moving, when other shadows are motionless. It is dodging frantically and is more conspicuous than the substance it depends upon for its existence, whose redness blends so subtly with the sand.

The pilot also sees the shadow and Johnson holds up his pen to show that the entry has been made. Abruptly, the plane noses down and Johnson glimpses a fleck of yellow as a red kangaroo appears in a split-second and is gone.

When they have pulled out of the shallow dive and are again in level flight along the final transect the pilot twists around and points meaningly at his neck. Sam gives an emphatic nod in reply; in making out his report that night he mentions the sighting of the kangaroo with a yellow collar, stating the exact position and adding that he understands Cable of the Australian Department of Industrial Research (Rural Division) has been doing some work involving identification by means of different-colored plastic collars.

When last sighted the identifiable red kangaroo buck was eighty kilometers due west of the earth tank where he had been captured and released when a member of Wangarie's group. During his drift westward he must have passed a bare and rocky ridge where the study of a different kind of kangaroo—the wallaroo—another N.P. & W.S. project under the control of Sam Johnson, had by then been in progress for some months.

October

OCTOBER STARTS as a gentle month.

Of the kangaroos feeding in the middle of an open plain, both Wangarie and the other blue flyer have pouch young. Wangarie's latest offspring is about six months old, the younger flyer is half that age.

There are five kangaroos not counting the two pouched joeys; three of the five who are old enough to have freedom of movement—Wangarie, Merloo, and the second of the blue flyers—are probably held together by a blood relationship. Wangarie is unquestionably the nucleus of the group, which, however, has no real leader. Merloo, of course, is still at heel to Wangarie, and the other blue flyer is almost certainly one of her elder daughters who did not break away on reaching maturity and is now keeping close from sheer force of habit.

At only fourteen months the last of the three does has transferred her attention from the blue flyer marked by one of Cable's white collars to Wangarie and seems to have become as continually aware of her as she had been of her own mother before their separation.

So it seems that Old Man Red is the only truly independent member of the group, and he always gives the impression that he could join up with any passing company, small or large, at any time. Sometimes he disappears for days and is often no more than an indistinct shape far across the plain. Nor do the others ever seek his company as he works his way gradually toward them or wanders off again, lazily, on another tack.

The attention Wangarie gives her latest joey is unflagging now that he has grown sufficiently to be recognized as a separate entity. She has taken progressively more notice of him from the day he first looked out of her pouch and is continually licking him from head to foot, whereas formerly she had cleaned him and her pouch only two or three times in twenty-four hours.

Now that he is trying to stand up by himself she is showing even more concern for the tremulous little creature whose wobbly legs cannot yet properly support him, whose heavy head is balanced on his neck as uncertainly as his meager body is balanced on his legs, and whose great liquid eyes seem to be bulging from their sockets as they goggle about in helpless uncomprehension. Anything easier for any predator, from an eagle to a goanna, to tear to pieces would be hard to imagine. Wangarie licks him on the side of the neck and, as he reels back from the thrust of her tongue, steadies him with her forepaws.

The grass where the kangaroos are resting is not as tall as in most other places. It is possible to see a few sheep farther across the paddock, also some gray foresters who have come to the edge of the mulga scrub and are sitting up as motionless as the weathered stumps of the trees they closely resemble.

An ibis glides overhead, its white wings translucent against the sun and, on the ground, a flock of gray birds with brown wings, known sometimes as the twelve apostles and sometimes as the happy family, are running through the grass. They fly into a leopard wood then glide to the ground again and run toward the trees of a sand ridge, chattering all the while and darting from side to side to snap up the insects disturbed by their exuberance.

Rolling to his feet, the red buck sends out a shower of dirt particles and dead grass stalks. He scratches his flanks noisily, takes an undecided hop, noses the ground, and settles down again, staring into the sunset under half-closed lids. Far off, a raven lets out a throaty *craack*, which, for some contradictory reason, does not mar the peace of that idyllic day.

The hot, drying winds of September are forgotten in the breezes that drift across the grasslands as mildly as cloud shadows. Or, if their timid rufflings should brighten the plains instead of darkening them because of a different angle of the light, there will always be a sparkling in the distance like the flurry that moves across a lake when a school of fish is swimming near its surface. Often on such days when the hour is past noon there is a profound quiet, and the air takes on a golden tint so that the sun seems to be shining down through deep, clear water onto a vast sea-meadow.

Every day is followed by another much the same, yet drowsier and more peaceful than its predecessor. Merloo and the daughter of the white-collared doe sometimes skitter wildly through the grass, but none of the other kangaroos displays much energy.

Merloo, on one occasion, shapes up to a young buck from a larger mob passing by. He gets the worst of the sparring match but trails after the strangers for an hour or more before going back to Wangarie.

The day soon comes when the soft airs of spring are brusquely swept away by a blast that bends the grass almost to the ground and sets the trees on the open plain swirling, and the longer the gale lasts the more restless the kangaroos become. They are always changing from place to place, trying to find shelter. The wind is so strong that they try to keep exactly head on to it—and then it hurts their eyes until the tears run down.

Wangarie's pouched joey will not venture out while the wind is whistling; Merloo and the others lie flat to the ground when resting and crouch as low as possible to feed.

Already brown and dry from the similar visitation of a month earlier, the grass and bushes quickly lose the small amount of moisture they have absorbed in the last few weeks, and the risk of fire is renewed. Nor does the wind abate except, sometimes, at night.

It is by day, however, that the return to danger is most apparent. Faint smoke clouds stain the sky perhaps twenty kilometers away, and there are sometimes black columns closer at hand.

Temperatures rise until they are about equal to mid-summer, and the dryness and heat combined are sufficient to blacken leaf buds on the windward sides of the trees. But there are still green shoots appearing around the bases of some of the grass tufts, as these are mostly in partial shade and protected from the wind. They usually develop a stem before being browned off. Merloo, who has lived solely by grazing in the last two months, spends each day searching for these green shoots and sometimes visits the edges of the scrub to browse on emu bush and budda.

The red kangaroos are taken by surprise by the first of the fires, which comes through the mulga, driven by the wind. They see its smoke billowing but do not move at once. Some of the red kangaroos have wandered far into the scrub with the gray foresters, and one of these is the blue flyer with the white collar. Since becoming separated from the group, she has been feeding where thickets of mulga and frequent open spaces combine to present a tremendous risk of fire.

In company with some gray foresters the blue flyer with the white collar has been bounding along at full speed for half an hour. But she is not as adept as the foresters at dodging around or between the innumerable mulga trees, and she is falling behind. The foresters are not only agile but strong. They can zig-zag like wallaroos and are nearly as tough, often barging right through a bush or hitting a projecting branch with a crash that never seems to hurt them or slow them down.

Although she, too, is traveling fast, the blue flyer has no room for her wonderful, smooth-flowing speed. It is race ahead, check, dodge, bound high, check and dodge again, flash along a straight alleyway, dodge, bound aside, zig-zag past yet more and more mulga trees, an endless forest of mulga trees with the crashings of the gray foresters becoming fainter ahead and the roar of the fire growing louder behind. Smoke driven by the wind has turned the sunlight to sulfur yellow, and every now and then accumulations of tinder-dry brushwood, catching alight, drown out the roar of the greater conflagration with the sounds of explosions. It is clear that the flyer, caught out of her natural habitat, is failing fast.

To worsen the situation she is burdened with a joey nearly old enough to be at foot, and as her flight becomes wilder through weakness and frequent collisions he suddenly goes rolling along the ground beside her. By the time he gets unsteadily to his feet she has gone.

She is so nearly spent she hardly knows what is happening. There is suddenly fire everywhere as those outriders of disaster, the wind-blown sparks, fall into the trees around her. Dead grass and branches on the ground, too, and the dry spinifex tufts as tall as she catch alight. She doubles frantically, but all the world is aflame and she falls, her fur blazing, and does not move again. Her white collar flares, melts, sputters viciously, and is consumed.

Wangarie, Old Man Red, and the rest of the group watch the glare reflected in the smoke hanging over the bush but do not appear to be greatly disturbed by the spectacle. Smoke and the setting sun give the western sky the appearance of a vast inferno.

As soon as the fire reaches the end of the scrubland countless sparks, launched by the violent updraft and carried by the wind, settle on the plains like flocks of scarlet birds, and the grass is alight in a hundred places.

The kangaroos, now hidden in smoke, now lit by flames, are thrown into a frenzy. None of them has yet escaped, for the burning patches are so widespread that in the confusion of flying from one threat they are always confronted by another.

Wangarie, followed by Merloo, streaks away at full speed only to turn again. At last she flashes through a gap to the darkening plain. She has lost Merloo, and the weight of her young one drags at her pouch each time her sinewy hind legs propel her forward.

Behind her the others have also escaped, the red buck with a burned heel, which does not affect his speed since his heels touch the ground only when he is sitting or crawling. He soon catches up with Wangarie, who has stopped to look back.

There is no great updraft now, nor will there be while only grass is burning. But grass fires are persistent and they keep widening their front. Eventually the kangaroos move around the fire, although it continues to make some ground in every direction except west, where a swath has been burned through the scrub.

For the next few days the red kangaroos are kept constantly on the move. They have re-formed as a group, and as they are now only being harassed and are not really panicked they also stay together.

Some gray foresters, too wary to return to their own habitat in case of further scrub fires, are at present wandering the plains in search of grass, they as well as Wangarie and her co-travelers now similarly black to their bellies. Large areas of country have so far escaped the flames and the landholders have made firebreaks around some of these.

Wangarie and the others hang around the earth tanks, drinking fairly often and feeding on the dead and withered grass stalks that in many instances have been beaten flat by stock coming in to drink. Merloo is the most fearful of the smoke that rises in the distance by day and the flames that glare at him by night. Wangarie and he are three kilometers from the tank when their paddock catches fire. A wind is blowing, and they are forced to retreat toward the comparative safety of the tank and its beaten-down surroundings.

Somewhat reassured by Wangarie's easy loping pace, Merloo is merely anxious, not agitated, although he keeps looking back to make sure the fire is not gaining. Ahead of them the red buck is rising above the grass tops only at the highest point of each bound. Merloo can hear the swish of his progress, the regular thuds of his landings. Too lazy or too shrewd to jump high, the big kangaroo is leaving a wake of downswept grass stems that start to recover immediately.

The blaze drives the fugitives toward the corner of the paddock where there is a homestead and outbuildings. The wings of the fence's corner are hung with sheepskins, flesh side up. Firebreaks have been burned around the enclosure, but the place seems deserted—until the figure of a woman shows momentarily through the wire-screened back door of the house.

As the three kangaroos approach the fence the broken rhythm of their thudding pads—one heavy and two light—is punctuated by the loudest thump yet, the red buck rising way above the others to see what lies on the other side of the sheepskins. Wangarie and Merloo pass him as he veers away. They rush the fence, and Merloo hits it with a twanging of wires. He lands clumsily, recovers, and excitedly turns on speed to catch up with the blue flyer. She has skimmed the obstruction like a bird and is covering the ground effortlessly at a brisk, unvarying pace.

Having turned away from the fence, the red buck now finds the fire pretty close to him. But he seems to have its measure and alters course again for the corner. He approaches the sheepskins at right angles as though determined to smash through but then takes a higher leap to check his landing place. Two more bounds and he is over without waste of energy and with a precision truly admirable in such a heavy animal.

Of course, he does not catch up with Wangarie in spite of the weight she is carrying. Her young one has not ventured to look out of her pouch since the flight from the grass fires began. Wangarie is drawing steadily away from Merloo. The grass beyond the fence is tall, and the young buck is finding the going tough.

The red kangaroos stop at the earth tank, but they do not graze. They sit up, licking their sweating forearms like big cats. They drink the muddy water of the tank. It smells of ash, tastes of ash, and is sprinkled with ash. All the stock has been moved from this paddock, and no animal besides the kangaroos comes to drink.

It is a fine night: hot, dry, and reeking of smoke. But no fire is visible until the fire the kangaroos have outdistanced works its way around a burned area and comes in from the side. It is moving slowly, in front of a faint breeze.

Crimson reflections glint from those parts of the tank not blanketed by ash, and Wangarie jumps to her feet as a tussock of wallaby grass flares like a torch. Her joey, who has been lying beside her, tries unsuccessfully to scramble back into her pouch, and it is not at once that she stoops forward to allow him in. He is very big and, until he settles himself, both his hind feet and his tail protrude. Another such flight as the last and he may not be alive to see the end of it. The blue flyer has been escaping from grass fires now for days and is too weary to carry him much farther. Her muscles have stiffened, too, after the rest. Nearby the red buck is drawn up to his full height ready to go. Merloo hops over the mound of the tank toward the plains and also sits up waiting. His eyes glow like fanned coals, now bright red, now dull, according to the antics of the flames.

Tension is lessening, but Wangarie remains watchful. Ears pricked, she too is sitting bolt upright, her pouch an ungainly bulge in her otherwise slender outline. An owl winnows by in search of small prey, but the fire is dying down, momentarily at any rate. It only just survives in the flattened grass. It divides to pass the tank and the southern wing goes out. The other runs along the edge of a bare claypan and the darkness widens. Then the flames stretch up in the long grass farther on, and gradually become fainter with distance.

The kangaroos go back to the top of the earth heaped around the tank and lie down as before. Wangarie's young one stays in her pouch.

When the month is halfway through, a gray bank of rain sweeps in from the west. The smell of wood ash and burned grass increases in bitterness for a while, but the kangaroos who had fled from the fires are back again within a week, nosing the ground for grass shoots.

November

WANGARIE'S DAUGHTER hops slowly across a claypan to the edge that was farthest from the wind when the fire passed. When she has cropped the grass growing there, she returns to the center of the claypan and lies down near the indifferent Wangarie. It is nearly dark and there has been a sudden drop in temperature.

The blue flyers have been resting for most of the day. The younger of the two has suffered more harassment from the fires than the other; this has already caused the failure of her milk supply through fatigue and brought about the death of her empouched young one.

Activated by the cessation of suckling consequent upon her loss, the dormant blastocyst in the second of her uteri has just started to develop. It will be ready to be born in thirty-one days.

With the destruction of so much feed and natural scrub cover, the gray foresters have become as easy to hunt as the red kangaroos and they also, or many of them, are in search of safer territory. Meanwhile all are obliged to forage in shallow gullies and other damp, eroded places for pockets of green grass and, perhaps, a scattering of small bushes that may have escaped the flames.

Concentrations of kangaroos always being profitable subjects for the shooters' spotlights, there are some big tallies marked up while the country around about is recovering. It is some time before the mobs start to disperse.

A hundred or so kilometers farther out there have been no fires, there being nothing to burn, and no rain. That is where Sam Johnson of the National Parks and Wildlife Services, camped at the foot of a rocky outcrop, is nearing the end of his study of wallaroos. In his opinion, the locality is eminently suitable for his investigation since it is a good example of a semi-arid area where a policy of deliberate overstocking has been put into effect in order to destroy the native shrubs and make possible the growing of more grass. To begin with, sheep thrived on this land—as did the kangaroos—after additional drinking places had been provided by the graziers and a favorable season had brought on the pasture. But continued heavy stocking together with an influx of kangaroos and a severe dry spell resulted in a collapse of the food supply. The red kangaroos cleared out, those sheep that were not withdrawn died, and only the wallaroos hung on, although it seemed there were not enough wisps of straw left to keep a grasshopper alive.

Of the three big kangaroos the gray foresters generally enjoy the kindest habitat, ranging from forest country to sparse, dry scrubland. By comparison the red kangaroos of the plains had to work harder to sustain life in drought times—until man dotted their territories with waterholes and sowed better grasses. Now, over much of their range, red kangaroos seldom depend for their lives on their kidneys, which are capable of producing urine containing such a high concentration of waste matter that the total amount of fluid voided is extraordinarily small.

Oddly, the urine of wallaroos is less concentrated than that of red kangaroos, although wallaroos live in the driest of habitats, often on the fringe of the desert. Also, they drink less than red kangaroos. In fact, it seems that some wallaroos never drink at all, evidently maintaining the moisture of their bodies by spending the daytime hours in their home caves or deep clefts in the rocks. By contrast, the best shelter a red kangaroo can hope to find is the shade of a tree; in semi-arid country he is sometimes obliged to lie all day in the open.

Wallaroos never inhabit any place where there is no escape from heat, and even in mildly warm weather they seldom appear before nightfall. Late on a cool afternoon, perhaps, they may venture out, especially if they are near the coast, but not in the inland during any of the nine hot months, not ever.

Inland wallaroos are stocky and tough. Their fur is mostly a dark brick red that seems black at a distance, except in sunshine. Sometimes it is black. Their legs are thick and powerful—so much so that they bounce rather than bound. They are immensely strong, their forelimbs particularly so in comparison with the slenderer arms of the red and the forester.

Wallaroos are solitary animals, and although several may gather together at some feeding ground or drinking place there is never any cohesion among them. They intermingle freely and then, having fed or drunk, go their own ways. The bucks often battle fiercely over females in oestrus, but when the fight is over and mating has taken place the animals concerned show no further interest in each other.

Sam Johnson has trapped and identified most of the wallaroos living in the granite outcrop he has selected for his research. There are two rock holes and a pool just beyond the scree at the bottom of a slope, but the three drinking places are so close together that he decided there was nothing to be gained from learning which wallaroos drink at which point. He covered the two rock holes with netting, erected a stout, two-and-a-half-meter-high wire fence around the pool, and fitted a trap gate.

All the animal tracks found by Johnson suggest there is no other water in the area, and the flight lines of birds point to the same conclusion. He has watched the birds from many places since his arrival, and the pattern of their comings and goings has always been consistent with his theory.

It has become a habit with him to sit in the shade of his camp in the late afternoon to listen for the budgerigars flying in to drink. He put some dead branches in the pool and never tires of the sudden hubbub of warbling cries as the first-comers flash into view over the rocks to the north and, wheeling as one, come fluttering down.

When the corellas and more budgerigars materialize out of the hot sky, the air is filled with wings as the parrots struggle to perch where there is room for only half their number. Clamor builds on clamor and confusion on confusion until the din is indescribable; in the midst of it all, though, a pair of crested pigeons may land and, having walked composedly to the water's edge, drink and fly away again. It is almost dark when the last of the birds leave and the feathers that have been sailing the ruffled surface of the pool seem to be as fixed as the land and sky around them.

Sam Johnson's first task after he and his helper had set up camp at the site four months ago had been to fit a collar on every wallaroo trapped. His records over this period showed that some animals visited the waterhole about once a week, some every ten days or so, others at intervals of four or five weeks.

Then, one night after his helper had returned to district headquarters, Sam Johnson took a flashlight and in the course of a two-hour prowl of known feeding places discovered ten wallaroos without collars. The next night he went to the other side of the outcrop and found five more, which meant that at least fifteen animals had not visited the waterhole over the period of the test so far. Since the nearest wallaroo community was thirty kilometers away and since, in any case, wallaroos are the "stay-puts" of the marsupial species, Johnson was certain the unidentified wallaroos had not come in from outside.

Nor do the records he is keeping please him in other of their aspects, since experiments he has carried out elsewhere with red kangaroos have shown him that some individuals are definitely less timid than others. He remembers that, formerly, after a drinking place had been fenced off for the study of red kangaroos some of the animals became quite used to being confined. In the present instance a wallaroo doe with a green-and-white plastic collar is caught every fourth or fifth night. She never shows any agitation, whereas a buck trapped about once a month always charges the fence headlong as soon as the men appear and, when he is finally released, bounces away up the cliffs at

tremendous speed. That particular wallaroo, Johnson feels
sure, would never visit the waterhole until his thirst had
become unbearable. The doe, on the other hand, would
probably drop in for a drink whenever she felt like it. In
Johnson's opinion such unavoidable variations in behavior
should be kept in mind in the drawing of conclusions from
even the most carefully collected and tabulated data.

Once again, the buck wallaroo has been captured, this
time nearly six weeks after his previous capture. Once
more he is plunging about the yard like a mad thing.
Johnson opens the gate as he crashes into a slim steel post,
bending it. Ricocheting off the wire he hits the gate post,
recovers, and tears like a cannon ball through the other
wallaroos making their way more rationally uphill. Vanishing among the shattered crags high up he follows a path
whose rocky points have been polished bright by genera-
tions of his kind. He dives downhill to push between the
two parts of a great monolith that has been split by the ice
of a frosty mid-winter night or by its own weight and scur-
ries on, now brushing hard against the dim-shining walls
of a chasm scarcely wide enough to admit him. Halfway
along this natural corridor one side of the rock has split
again, and again the black buck wallaroo, his pads scuffing
the smooth floor under him, squeezes through a crevice.
There is now no glint of sunshine and not much light. But
it is in here, in the cool dark stinking of male wallaroo,
that he will sleep away the day. The silence is not broken
until a hawk alights on a peak late in the afternoon to send
its shrill, incisive cry threading into the shafts and hollows
of the pile.

The wallaroo does not emerge until long after the sun
has set. Rock surfaces gleam under a high-riding moon,

and the arid, sandy waste, blotched with the shadows of a few bushes, is a picture of desolation. The buck wallaroo sits up, motionless. Dry, acrid scents of the desert come faintly to his sensitive nostrils. He waits, as though turned to stone, as every other thing within sight seems to be doing. Then he drops down on all fours and picks his way slowly down the tumble of rock to level ground.

Johnson's study is almost at an end. If he has made no new discovery at least he has confirmed a lot of what has already been observed about the species.

He has taken measurements, determined the age of his captives by inspecting their teeth, gauged the rate of growth of their young, noted the incidence of their visits to the drinking pool, and tabulated much of his recorded work. He has confirmed what he was pretty sure of before—that wallaroos do not live much longer than ten to twelve years at best under harsh conditions, that the rate of growth of the young varies according to the conditions, that they drink from twice a week to about once a year, that they never emerge in daylight if the weather is hot, that they never leave their home range in a dry time but may wander farther afield if there is plenty of feed, and that, all in all, they are ideally adapted for living in rocky or mountainous country from the coast to the desert edge.

Now that he has shot six animals and forwarded their stomachs to Sydney for examination he has only to await the outcome of his final experiment with a buck and a doe wallaroo encaged near his camp. After six weeks without water the doe's young-at-heel has died and now, after another month, both she and the buck are weak and emaciated. Other such tests he had read about had ended at ninety days and it seems that this one will end there also. The doe is skin and bone, the buck almost too feeble to stand, and Johnson is full of misgivings.

He has been feeding them their natural food, the food he knows they eat and which he gathers from the wasteland around him. This seems to imply that he is as skilled at finding moisture-rich food as they would be, but he does not believe that. How many succulents would they find if they were roaming free? More than he can find? He has not found any. What is the natural food of wallaroos dying of thirst? And would they continue to stay at home if things got as bad as that or would they migrate? Anyway, they certainly would not spend their days above ground in the heat and drying wind as they are obliged to do while in a cage. What about the wild wallaroos that were never caught in the yard built around the pool? Some of them had not drunk for the duration of his study.

A few years ago he had witnessed a population explosion of sheep and wallaroos after additional water points had been provided by graziers in a semi-arid district of West Australia. A tremendous growth of grass had sprung up after a wonderful fall of rain. The number of sheep had been greatly increased, and there then came a normal dry season, the disappearance of the grass, the withdrawal of some of the sheep, and the death by starvation of others as well as of thousands of wallaroos. Yet there had been something inevitable about that disaster. It was different with the two caged wallaroos lying out in the open and weakening gradually to their inevitable end.

Two days later he fills their food can with water in a fit of absentmindedness and leaves the door of their cage open by accident. When he has loaded the last pieces of gear into the truck he returns to Sydney. His detailed report on a male and female wallaroo kept without water says both were at the point of death when they escaped, which is true—in a way.

Shooting outfits, a few operating from mobile chillers but most of them engaged in the reduction of kangaroo numbers by permission of special licenses issued for particular areas, are obtaining high tallies of gray forester and red kangaroos on some properties recently swept by fire, for feeding grounds are now few and far between—although the grass is starting to regenerate where thunderstorms have occurred.

Wangarie's group has traveled northwest to a property where there is at present no shooting.

The owner of the property has always had some red kangaroos inside his boundaries and some grays in a forested corner of his station. He has no objection to supporting a certain number of kangaroos, although he admits they can become a nuisance. The foresters have to be thinned out occasionally. So far he has never permitted the shooting of any reds. He is somewhat concerned about the future of the red kangaroo, the more so since being counseled by a friend to take the sensibly unemotional view—to be on the safe side and shoot them all.

He has not, yet, ever felt obliged to follow that advice, although he admits that totals fluctuate. Some animals leave occasionally for better pastures, and others enter his property—as has a group of five, today, from some part of the fire-swept country outside.

December

Owing to a providential change in the direction of the wind the grasslands where Wangarie has been grazing recently are unburned. But the fire danger is as acute as ever. Moisture from recent rain has been sucked up by long hours of sunshine, and the day is the fourth of a heat wave.

Thirty or so kangaroos have been lying under some trees since dawn, and the sun is past its zenith. Some of the younger animals, Merloo among them, change from one patch of shade to the next as the mood strikes them, but the older kangaroos seem to be prostrated by the heat. Only their ears, pygmy creatures with lives of their own, are active.

Slumber, deep slumber, is rare among kangaroos, but one aged buck is certainly asleep. Yet his ears are alert, and the ears of a blue flyer drowsing near him twitch and turn like mechanical listening devices, scanning the distances. Not that there is much to be picked up except the rustling of grasshoppers in flight and the desiccated click-click of their melodies.

The kangaroos are on a plain east of the Darling and about eighty kilometers from Cobar where they are not likely to be disturbed, for their location is remote for the region—which makes the plain's resemblance to an immense park curious, not to say unreal.

The expanse of silvery brown grass is so level that it might have been mown; the wilga and leopard woods look as though they had been planted. Perhaps the wilgas do most to bring about the parklike effect, because they are naturally rounded above and neatly trimmed below for as high as a sheep can reach.

Mid-afternoon and the heat is no less. A willy willy spins up from the edge of an earth tank and, eddying on, becomes a whirlwind of dust and flying straw. Silhouetted against her sunswept background, a blue flyer sits up to lick her forearms, her head moving up and down like a cat's; from a branch above her a discordant scream towers so powerfully into the hot skies that it is some moments before the silence it leaves behind effervesces once more into the buzzing of insects. A raven planes to the mound encircling the earth tank. His plumage glitters like black armor. When he has drunk he flies an undeviating course out of sight.

As the red, expanding sun touches the horizon a flock of corellas comes fluttering down to the tank, and the oppressive hush is briefly enlivened by the cries of the birds and the flash of wings. A platoon of sheep files through the dusk to form a curved rank at the edge of the water, and the strong smell of them is the smell that was detectable before they arrived. They do not wait but, having drunk, return the way they came. When their bleatings and the sound of their hard little hoofs clip-clipping along the track have faded, the evening is very quiet. The mound of earth around the tank radiates heat.

Kangaroos from two or three kilometers away take shape out of the dusk, and there are soon ten or twelve of them watchfully drinking. A full-grown buck trails Wangarie. His way is immediately barred, however, by Old Man Red, and the strange buck looks away and noses the ground as though in search of grass where there is none for fifty meters in any direction.

Stopping under a leopard wood, Wangarie adopts the birth position of the red kangaroo by leaning against the trunk of the tree in a sitting attitude with her tail stretched forward between her hind legs. A tendency to roll sideways is checked by the pressure of her back against the tree. But she does not remain quiet and is soon wandering around restlessly. She assumes the birth position again; this happens three or four times before, an hour or so later, the neonate finally appears. Once started, the birth and the journey to the pouch are over in a few minutes. It is the second December birth within the group so far, Wangarie's daughter having produced a young one earlier in the month.

After an assiduous licking and cleaning process in which the glistening, snaillike trail left by the tiny sleepwalker is cleared away, the blue flyer quits the dusty patch under the tree for the open plain. While she was in shadow the moon was rising, and now the night is luminous. Grazing animals are scattered sparsely around the earth tank.

When viewed from their lighted side kangaroos are less no-
ticeable than sheep. They move more slowly and huddle
so low to the ground when feeding that they look like
bushes.

Wangarie's young-at-heel, now denied access to her
pouch in case he should crush the new occupant, crowds
anxiously against his mother; Merloo, who has not been
suckled for nearly five months, is also close enough to be
considered in their company. He is as tall as Wangarie and
well-grown, but he still likes to keep her in sight. At
present, this is an easy matter because of the brightness of
the light. The night, in fact, could be said to be another,
although less ardent, day—a wide and peaceful scene lit by
a mammoth moon and oppressed for all its beauty by the
same unrelenting heat.

It is not until the early hours of the morning that the big
buck who attached himself to the group last March begins
to hover around Wangarie. But she shows no sign of ac-
cepting his advances then or, indeed, at any hour of that
day, and it is the following evening before Old Man Red,
resuming his courtship after an interval of somnolence, re-
ceives a favorable response. His attentions quickly become
more urgent, a development that brings Wangarie's joey-
at-heel many an accidental bump and finally drives him
from his mother's side.

In marked contrast with the lethargy of the other
kangaroos in the heat wave, the old buck is now so intent
on the pursuit of the blue flyer that he fails to see his
former challenger drawn up to his full height in the dap-
pled shade of a leopard wood. But Wangarie sees him and
promptly veers away.

Heads thrown back and arms raking the air the bucks confront one another, and the challenger advances in a series of short, shuffling hops into the glare of the moon. When they are some six or seven meters apart they drop down on all fours in another of the preliminaries to battle—the attempt to intimidate by presenting a wide and forbidding front with expanded chest and arms aggressively thrust sideways to display the veins, muscles, and sinews of the upper body corded under extreme tension. The whole performance is further dramatized by continuous quiverings of the frame and the baring of teeth. Nor is there any doubt about their ferocity. Their eyes are aflame and their guttural coughings and growlings extraordinarily loud for animals usually so quiet. The stranger also uses an additional means of threatening his opponent—a furious sibilance, like the turning-on of a steam jet and made by forcing saliva out between his clenched teeth under pressure and then sucking it in again.

Not that either has yet shown any sign of alarm at the other's performance. In fact, there is a lull in the affair at this moment while the two bucks, having demonstrated their great width of chest, resume the erect position to demonstrate their height. Old Man Red is slightly the taller when they are standing on their toes, and the stranger would overtop a tall man by a head. Since both are stretched up to the limit, both look extremely attenuated. Their chests are drawn up high, their arms move like boxers', and their bellies are as part of their long, slim waists. The moonlight limns one side of them with a silvery glow of fur.

Muscles tautened by their great excitement are jerking

their limbs into the most grotesque attitudes, and the arms of the challenger start to vibrate wildly, crossing and un-crossing as his head is forced back as though by a convul-sion. Saliva pours from his mouth, and the sinews of his neck go into spasm. Old Man Red is rent by similar parox-ysms. They are like two big clockwork figures whose mechanisms have gone wrong. Suddenly, they squat back on their haunches, gasping for breath and dribbling over their forearms.

The next stage of the confrontation uses up as much energy as the last, although no blow has yet been struck. They rasp furiously at their chests and again tighten every muscle to the limit of its strength. Sometimes, as though by common consent, there are even more definite breaks in these preliminaries to battle—if there is to be a battle— and often the contestants will draw apart while they lick their forearms. Their wrists have been drenched with sweat since soon after the start of the display, and it is on their wrists and forearms, where a fine network of blood vessels lies close to the surface of the skin, that they keep slobber-ing in order to cool themselves. Kangaroos do not sweat from any other part of their bodies, a provision which, in the present situation, would seem to be more than offset by the amount of saliva already lost by both animals.

Whenever the posturings stop it is with great sudden-ness, and when they start again it is just as suddenly. Even after the duel has been in progress for over two hours nei-ther kangaroo shows any inclination to avoid the next clash, although it is now clear that both are in distress. Their breathing has been reduced to gasping, the harsh cries and coughs of their earlier displays to an occasional grunt of rage.

It is amazing the way the bucks, no matter how winded they may seem when resting, always perform so frenziedly as soon as they come to close quarters again. They cannot maintain the pace, of course, but, as in the present encounter, it is certainly furious while it lasts as, with backbones strenuously recurved, they start another round by striking at each other's eyes. It is their first attempt to injure—not that there is actually much danger to their sight, for the rule that heads must always be kept as far as possible out of harm's way is never broken.

So the sharp claws are always falling short of the real target with the result that the adversaries keep on raking one another's chest, from the base of the throat down. Within minutes, the fur of the upper fronts of their bodies is a sodden mess of blood and saliva, and the fighters are again close to exhaustion. Their movements are slower and weaker, their breathing is growing steadily louder, and both are showing the effects of severe dehydration in the great heat. Saliva is still stringing down from mouths slack with fatigue. If this is to be a fight to a finish—and that is the way it looks at the moment—then it seems likely that the finish will be the collapse of the loser.

The contenders reel apart and the bigger of the two, Old Man Red, is first to recover. He draws himself up to his full height and, supported momentarily by his tail alone, kicks out so powerfully with his hind legs that his enemy is dashed to the ground. It is the only solid blow so far, but the advantage is not followed up.

Nevertheless, it seems the fight is over. Old Man Red licks his forearms and his bloodied chest. The other, apparently, is too nearly spent to move. But at last, slowly and dazedly, the prostrate buck starts to get to his feet.

After a while the victor hops toward Wangarie, whereupon the challenger instantly cuts across his path and, standing on the tripod of hind toes and tail, again prepares to do battle. Both are rocking on their feet before the new display has properly begun, and the affair peters out.

Old Man Red crawls slowly and painfully to the earth tank and drinks. When he returns his rival is stretched out on the grass, yet staggers to his feet again. If the former engagements were more vigorous, the present struggle is in its way more vicious because the original reason for the clash seems to have been lost in an enmity that has gradually become implacable—a surmise only made the more credible by the near-exhaustion of the fighters.

It is nearly morning and, in what is to be their last encounter, the two are locked together as boxers sometimes are at the end of a long and savage contest, when they are too weary to punch and each seems to be trying to overbear the other by sheer weight. Gaspings for breath and the shuffle of feet on the dry and slippery grass prevent the struggle from being absolutely silent, but it is so nearly so that some kangaroos nearby are already dozing in the hot, pre-dawn hush. The end comes when the stranger is suddenly pushed away, giving Old Man Red room to kick out with the little strength left to him. But it is enough, and the downfall of the challenger is absolute. Flung to earth he lies motionless, blood flowing from a rip in his belly.

The victor again approaches Wangarie. But she evades

him and, uncharacteristically, he does not persist. He is too tired to persist. He makes for the tank again, to drink.

As he crawls back over the mound to seek the shade, for it is now bright day, his defeated rival tries to regain his feet but cannot. A second attempt to climb the rise to get to the water is feebler than the first and, sinking down, he rolls over on his back. He is in the same place and attitude when the shadows have crept under the trees at noon, and although he seems to be staring defiantly at the sun-bleached sky, he is dead.

Having visited the earth tank in an interval between the many clashes that had occurred throughout the night, Old Man Red had been in very much better condition than his opponent during the last stages of the fight. It is probable that the loser, too, would have lived if he had been able to reach the water.

As for the surviving kangaroo, untroubled rest for him is not yet. Flies, swarms of them, are settling on the blood and moisture oozing from his chest and throat, and he is in torment. He strikes at them, but his skin is tender so he licks his chest and throws dust into the air. But they will not let him be and he is forever twitching and twisting, and tossing dust, and hitting his flanks and tail as well as his frontal parts. They attack him until he leaps to his feet in a frenzy and rips at the ground with his forepaws as a dog will when burying a bone. Dirt spatters his belly and chest as though sprayed from a power hose, the clods falling and the dust rising. He does this repeatedly but the cloud soon thins and when the flies come back his sufferings start again.

He revisits the tank in the early afternoon. The sun is at

its hottest, and he returns quickly to the deep shade. The flies are there, too, of course, but he endures them through extreme weariness—except the stinging ones. They always cause him to flinch and to reply with a slash of claws or an irritable nip, if his teeth can reach the affected part. Only once more that day is he bedeviled into that half-crazed digging up of the earth that will give him brief respite if the dust cloud raised is thick enough.

The ravens find the dead kangaroo before evening. There are three of them—there will be others tomorrow. Bold, yet wary, too, and tireless, they must surely be numbered among the strong ones of the world. The carcass shudders from the stabbings of their beaks.

When dusk falls a dog fox and a vixen succeed the ravens. They pause as the big red buck lumbers by on his way yet again to the tank. Dust shakes from his fur every time his hind legs thump the ground.

He returns to the plains, and the moon is rising as out of an ocean when he makes his next approach to Wangarie. The blue flyer moves away. When she stops to graze he paws at her and she turns on him angrily, slashing him across the muzzle. Flinging up his head and obviously fearing for his eyes, he backs off at once and starts to feed.

Very shortly, however, he returns to Wangarie and follows her about as before, repeatedly bumping into her, grabbing her neck and shoulders, and uttering a series of staccato clucking noises.

Wangarie retreats but does not actually repulse him, although she sometimes breaks her silence with a cry so loud and harsh that it sounds anything but amicable. Their fairly strenuous maneuvers last for about half an hour when the blue flyer suddenly comes to a stop and mating takes place.

Providing fertilization now occurs, another blastocyst will soon be lying dormant in the appropriate uterus of the blue flyer, there to await the peremptory summons to prepare to be born—a summons that could come literally at any moment if the empouched joey were to die prematurely or that could be delayed until it reaches that stage of its existence, in about seven months, when the sucking stimulus on its mother's teat will slacken sufficiently for the signal to be given by that means.

Blastocysts, presumably, have no consciousness, or the strain of being continuously on call throughout the earliest phase of their existence would reduce all kangaroos to nervous wrecks before they saw the light of day.

In the year coming to a close Wangarie has been successful in rearing one joey, Merloo, who is slowly gravitating toward the company of some young bucks of another group. He often spars with them at sunrise and sunset. The familiar shape and scent of Wangarie are now quickly fading from his memory.

Of the four blue flyers associated with the small group since the beginning of the year, two have died, together with their empouched joeys and young-at-heel, and two have survived. Wangarie is one of the survivors; the other, a younger blue flyer, is believed to be one of Wangarie's daughters. Wangarie herself has lost no offspring during the year, but the other blue flyer lost a joey-at-heel in August and a second, younger, joey that had not left her pouch when it died in October. The suckling at present in her pouch was born in the first week of December. So the mortality rate among young kangaroos has, as usual, been high.

The red kangaroos remain in the same place until the heat wave is over. Even then they travel only as far as a cluster of three rosewood trees, a scant five minutes' journey west. A track winds past the trees, and there are two shovels, a post-hole digger, and a crowbar lying beside it. The next day, the last of the year, late on a sunshiny afternoon, a stubby little utility truck comes into view, shimmering and wavering in the brilliance of the plains. It heads straight for the kangaroos.

If it had been a bright, cold afternoon in winter Old Man Red would not have delayed a moment. As it is, he is somewhat tardy. But go he does, after thumping loudly with his hind feet. Repeating the alarm, and then again, with a few bounds between signals, he settles down to a leisurely retreat. The others follow.

"They don't come much redder than that, not even out in the desert country," the driver of the utility remarks, as he pulls up alongside the collection of fencing tools.

He and his companion toss the gear aboard, and the sound of its clanging makes the kangaroos put on a spurt.

"Look at the flyer go," the driver adds to his previous observation.

Wangarie is now leading the small company and, having changed direction, is traveling only diagonally away from the watchers. Her blue pelt is as silky smooth as the hide of a well-groomed thoroughbred, and she seems to be floating along in undulating flight—as though the momentum of each descent were sufficient to send her away on the next bound. The white legs of her joey-at-heel flicker through the grass tops in their attempts to keep up. Merloo and the yearling doe follow, then the other blue flyer, who is more definitely blue after her annual molt than she was last year. There being no pursuit, the pace slackens.

Although the men have seen many hundreds of kangaroos they continue to watch before driving on. There is something about the scene besides its beauty and its space, the warm, clear air and sky, and the sweep of grass-lands gleaming in the sunset. They are aware of all these things subconsciously, and it is the kangaroos who hold their attention as they disappear one by one behind a sand ridge in the distance. At last, only Merloo is left. He stops and sits up and looks back. Then his head, so far away as to be scarcely distinguishable, seems to change its shape, and he too passes out of sight.

Conversion Table
Glossary
Bibliography
Index

Conversion Table

METRIC	U.S. EQUIVALENT
LENGTH	
centimeter	0.3937 inch
meter	3.2808 feet
	1.0936 yard
kilometer	0.6214 mile
WEIGHT	
kilogram	2.2046 pounds

Glossary

Apostle bird (*Struthidea cinerea*). Lively gray bird with black tail. Also called gray jumper and, because it is often found in small parties, the happy family or twelve apostles.

Bail up. To turn at bay.

Bandicoot (*Perameles nasuta*). The long-nosed bandicoot. A small insect-eating marsupial. Will also eat mice and small mammals.

Belah (*Casuarina cristata*). Tree with besomlike clusters of leafless branchlets. Sometimes called desert oak.

Blastocyst. A fertilized egg in the reproductive tract of the female red kangaroo; a very early stage of the embryo.

Blue flyer. Mature female of the red kangaroo species, *Megaleia rufa*. Its color is bluish gray in the great majority of cases.

Boomer. Very big—and, therefore, aged—buck kangaroo.

Box, bimble (*Eucalyptus populnea*). Eucalyptus with leaves that shimmer in the lightest breeze. Also called poplar box and shiny leaf box.

Budda (*Eremophila mitchellii*). Small tree of the inland areas. Carries purplish or white flowers in the spring.

Budgerigar (*Melopsittacus undulatus*). Small parrot of the semi-arid regions. Also called parakeet and lovebird.

Bull oak (*Casuarina luehmannii*). Small casuarina tree found in poor, sandy soils.

Casuarina. A group of trees remarkable for the virtual disappearance of their leaves. Includes swamp oak, river oak, she oak, bull oak, forest oak, desert oak, and belah.

Cockatoo, red-tailed black (*Calyptorhynchus magnificus*). Large cockatoo inhabiting much of coastal and inland Australia.

Cockatoo, white (*Cacatua galerita*). The sulfur-crested cockatoo, found in eastern part of Australia.

Coolabah (*Eucalyptus microtheca*). Eucalyptus with light gray foliage. Grows on black soil plains near rivers or underground water.

Corella (*Cacatua sanguinea*). The little corella. A small cockatoo that exists in great flocks in inland Australia.

Crab holes. Small holes that occur in the black soil plains. Dangerous to horses and riders.

Curlew, bush (*Burhinus magnirostris*). A bird, also known as the stone curlew. Its weird call is uttered mostly at night.

Dingo (*Canis familiaris dingo*). The warrigal or Australian wild dog.

Dog, kangaroo. Dog used for hunting kangaroos. Generally greyhound or part greyhound.

Dog, sheep. Smallish dog, usually a kelpie. Red kelpies resemble foxes. They are tireless workers and virtual nonbiters.

Eagle, wedge-tailed (*Aquila audax*). The wedgetail, one of the world's largest eagles.

Eagle, whistling (*Haliastur sphenurus*). A medium-size eagle.

Embryonic diapause. The prolonged storage of a dormant but viable embryo (blastocyst) in the reproductive tract of a lactating female kangaroo.

Emu (*Dromaius novae-hollandiae*). Flightless bird, second in size only to the African ostrich. The emu is found only in Australia, where it is distributed throughout grasslands, forests, and semi-arid areas.

Emu bush (*Eremophila longifolia*). A shrub of the inland that produces a small drupe, a favorite food of emus.

Falcon (*Falco* sp.). The peregrine, black, gray, and little falcons, are all found in the eastern parts of inland Australia.

Flyer. *See* Blue flyer.

Forester. *See* Kangaroo, forester.

Fox (*Vulpes vulpes*). The European fox, now widespread in Australia.

Fox, flying (*Pteropus* sp.). Giant fruit bats inhabiting the warm coastal regions.

Galah (*Eolophus roseicapillus*). A gray and rose-pink cockatoo of medium size. Occurs in large flocks on the grasslands of Australia.

Gilgai. A small hollow in a black soil plain where water collects after rain.

Goanna (*Varanus varius*). The common goanna or lace monitor. An omnivorus lizard growing to about two meters in length. Common in Australia.

Grass, kangaroo (*Themeda australis*). Native perennial tussock grass; grows tall in good seasons.

Grass, wallaby (*Danthonia* sp.). Native perennial grass of good nutrient value.

Grass, windmill (*Chloris* sp.). Tall native grasses, mostly perennial. Seeds are carried on radiating spokes. Also known as star grass and umbrella grass.

Gum, river red (*Eucalyptus camaldulensis*). A fine eucalyptus found growing along many inland rivers of the eastern third of Australia.

Hectare. 2.7 acres.

Ibis (*Threskiornis molucca*). The Australian white ibis or sickle bird.

Ironwood (*Acacia excelsa*). One of the larger trees of the plains. Grows to twenty meters.

Joey. A young kangaroo of either sex.

Kangaroo, forester (*Macropus giganteus*). Also gray forester, eastern gray, and great gray kangaroo. Both sexes are a medium gray color and have shaggier coats than red kangaroos. Foresters live in forest and scrub country. A large buck may stand over two meters high and weigh ninety to ninety-five kilograms, females about forty-five kilograms.

Kangaroo, red (*Megaleia rufa*). Also known as the plains kangaroo. A fully mature red kangaroo buck may top two and one-fourth meters when standing on his toes and the end of his tail. He could weigh ninety-five kilograms. The female, or blue flyer, is much smaller, weighing only about twenty-seven kilograms. Red kangaroos are remarkable for their wide color variations. They may be red or blue or any blend of those two colors. In western New South Wales, however, where the story is set, mature bucks are nearly always red and mature females nearly always blue or bluish gray. All red kangaroos have pale, whitish legs and black whisker marks. Their muzzles are light colored. Their natural habitat is the plains, and they live chiefly on grass.

Kangaroo, western gray (*Macropus fuliginosus*). Also known as the black-faced, sooty, and mallee kangaroo. This kangaroo is very much like the forester, or eastern gray, except that its color is brownish and the head and the end half of its tail are generally black or very dark gray. Its habitat is roughly southwest of the habitat of the eastern gray.

Kestrel (*Falco cenchroides*). The nankeen kestrel. Small hawk found all over Australia. It eats mice, grasshoppers, and large insects.

Kite, fork-tailed (*Milvus migrans*). A scavenger and bird of prey. Also known as the black kite.

Leopard, wood (*Flindersia maculosa*). Small tree of the inland. It has a spotted trunk.

Lignum (*Muehlenbeckia cunninghamii*). Tough native shrub that sometimes invades cleared lands to form tangled thickets. Prefers situations subject to periodic flooding. Often provides harborage for one of Australia's worst pests, the feral pig. Has some value as stock feed in drought.

Mulga (*Acacia aneura*). A large shrub or small to medium-size tree growing over large tracts of country in the inland. The grayish foliage makes excellent fodder, a good standby in droughts. Mulga woodlands, besides being extensive, are often very dense.

Neonate. A newborn animal.

Oak, river (*Casuarina cunninghamiana*). Tall casuarina that grows on river banks. Does not extend inland beyond eastern fringes of the plains.

Oestrus. Condition of sexual receptivity in the female; in heat. In the red kangaroo the length of the oestrous cycle averages thirty-five days.

Old man. Aged male kangaroo of the larger species. An outsized old man might be called a boomer.

Old man salt bush (*Atriplex* sp.). A small shrub growing in dry and semi-arid country. *See* Salt bush.

Owl, barking (*Ninox connivens*). Found in many parts of inland Australia. Also called the screaming-woman bird and the murder-bird.

Pademelon. Pronounced *paddymelon*. A small species of kangaroo. *Kangaroo* generally refers to the largest species, then come the wallabies, pademelons, hare wallabies, and rat kangaroos.

Pigeon, crested (*Ocyphaps lophotes*). Fawn and gray inland bird that has a black crest. Also called topknot pigeon.

Pigweed (*Portulaca* sp.). Fleshy, succulent plant that grows close to the ground after rain. Favorite food of kangaroos.

Pine, cypress (*Callitris columellaris*). A "pointed" tree that grows in dry situations on the coast and is also found, smaller and tougher, on the inland plains.

Quandong (*Santalum acuminatum*). Small tree of the inland. Also the small red fruit thereof.

Rat kangaroo, musky (*Hypsiprymnodon moschatus*). Very small inhabitant of the North Queensland rain forest and the only member of the kangaroo family to have five toes on its hind feet.

Raven (*Corvus coronoides*). Large bird of the crow family; omnivorous.

Rosewood (*Heterodendrum oleifolium*). Small, hardy tree of low-rainfall areas. Often stunted to shrub size. Also known as bullock bush, apple bush, and boonery.

Salt bush (*Atriplex* sp.). Perennial native plants that grow freely on the plains of the southeastern inland area. Acceptable feed for most herbivores.

Station. Large grazing property.

Stockman. Sheep (or cattle) herder.

Tank, earth. A scooped-out depression with sloping floor and hilled edges for water collection.

Teal (*Anas gibberifrons*). The gray teal. A wild duck.

Vixen (*Vulpes vulpes*). Mature female European fox.

Wallaby. Smaller species of kangaroo.

Wallaby, southern whiptail (*Wallabia parryi*). Inhabitant of the warm coastal forests. Sometimes known as the pretty-face.

Wallaroo (*Macropus robustus*). One of the larger kangaroos. Stockily built, powerful animal frequenting rough, rocky country in all regions of Australia. Very dark red or very dark gray in color. Appears black, even at a short distance. Also known as hill kangaroo, euro, and biggada.

Wedgetail. *See* Eagle, wedge-tailed.

Wee juggler (*Cacatua leadbeateri*). A very beautiful bird found in several localities throughout the southern half of inland Australia. Also known as Major Mitchell's cockatoo and pink cockatoo.

Wilga (*Geijera parviflora*). Small, shapely shade tree of the inland.

Willy-wagtail (*Rhipidura leucophrys*). Insectivorous bird, found throughout Australia. Also known as black-and-white fantail.

Willy willy. A summertime whirlwind often carrying dust, sticks, and larger debris high into the air.

Yarran (*Acacia homalophylla*). Small, open trees often growing in groups.

Bibliography

Anderson, R. H. *The Trees of New South Wales*. Sydney: Government Printer, 1968.

Cayley, Neville W. *What Bird Is That?* Sydney: Angus and Robertson, 1968.

Forshaw, Joseph M. *Parrots of the World*. Melbourne: Landsdowne Press, 1973.

Fox, A. M. "Kangaroos in New South Wales." Sydney: National Parks and Wildlife Service, 1974.

Frith, H. J., and Calaby, J. H. *Kangaroos*. Melbourne: F. W. Cheshire, 1969.

Holliday, Ivan, and Hill, Ron. *Field Guide to Australian Trees*. Adelaide: Rigby Ltd., 1969.

Ride, W. D. L. *A Guide to the Native Mammals of Australia*. Melbourne: Oxford University Press, 1970.

Troughton, Ellis. *Furred Animals of Australia*. Sydney: Angus and Robertson, 1968.

Wilson, George. "The Management of Kangaroos." Sydney: Parks & Wildlife, Vol. 1, No. 4.

Commonwealth Scientific & Industrial Research Organization. "The Birth of the Red Kangaroo." Division of Wildlife Research, Canberra.

Royal Zoological Society of New South Wales, Taronga Park, Mosman, Sydney. "Kangaroos and Men." A Symposium. The Australian Zoologist, Vol. XVI, Part 1, 1971.

Index

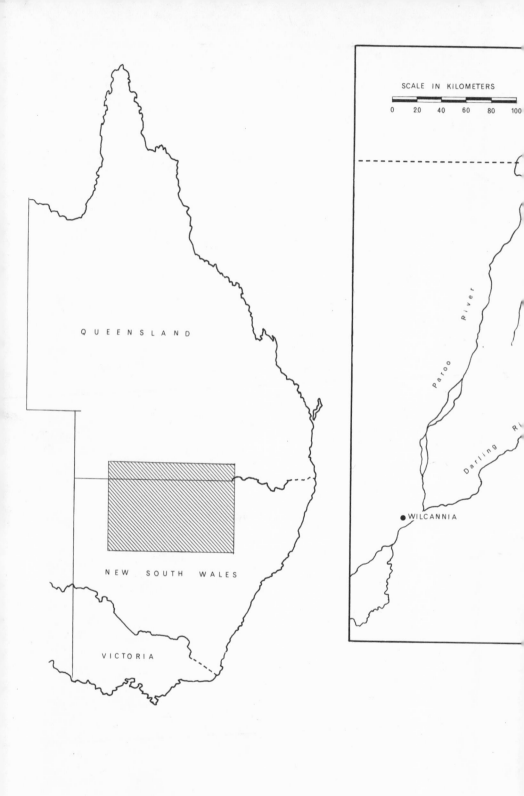